THE HEBRIDES
A Habitable Land?

J. Morton Boyd
and Ian L. Boyd

Birlinn

This Edition published in 1996 by
Birlinn Limited
14 High Street
Edinburgh EH1 1TE

The Publisher acknowledges subsidy from the Scottish Arts Council
towards the publication of this volume.

941·14
1296934

THE HEBRIDES
ISBN 1 874744 55 6–A Habitable Land? (Book I)
56 4–A Natural Tapestry (Book II)
57 2–A Mosaic of Islands (Book III)

A CIP record of this book is available
from the British Library

Printed and bound in Scotland by Bell & Bain Limited

THE HEBRIDES
A Habitable Land?

Map of the Hebrides

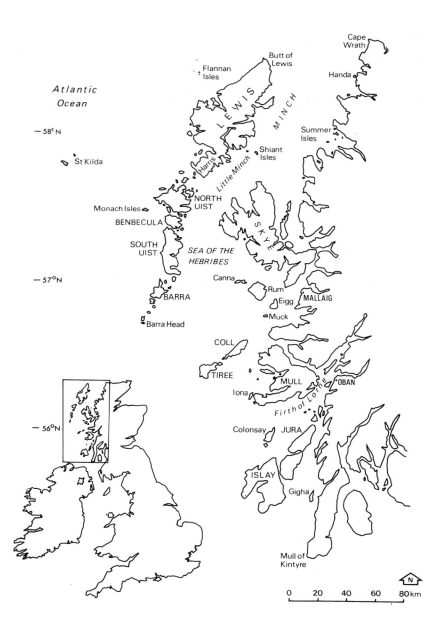

FOR EUAN

In the same day the Lord
made a covenant with Abram,
saying, unto thy seed have I
given this land . . .

Genesis 15:18

Contents

CONTENTS

Preface and Acknowledgements

The Hebrides—a habitable land? (H-AHL) is substantially Part III 'Islands and People' of the HarperCollins New Naturalist volume *The Hebrides—a natural history*. Chapters 1 and 6 are new, but the core of the book is Chapters 17–20 of that previous work. This book has two companions: *The Hebrides—a natural tapestry* (H-ANT) and *The Hebrides—a mosaic of islands* (H-AMI), which are respectively Parts I and II of that previous work. The three books now have independence, but their common origin in the New Naturalist volume, now out of print, gives them an interdependence as a comprehensive review of Hebridean natural history. This specific book deals with the human dimension of the natural history while the others deal with the structure of the archipelago (Volume 2) and the distribution of species among the islands (Volume 3).

Morton and Ian Boyd are a father and son team, and it could be said that the work of which this is a part has been forty years in the making. Morton might never have attempted it had he not collaborated with Fraser Darling in the writing of an earlier New Naturalist volume *The Highlands and Islands* in 1964. From the inside, as it were, he could see the great advantages of having the book written by a single author, not just for style of writing, but also for the artistry of compilation of a single comprehensive work from a wide variety of sources. The alternative is to compile a book with many experts contributing one or more chapters, but the result would be very different from the type of books produced by some of the authors of classical natural history books—F. Fraser Darling, E. B. Ford, C. M. Yonge, W. H. Pearsall, Dudley Stamp, Alistair Hardy and others in the New Naturalist series. These authors were at once experts in a limited field, and naturalists of broad erudition and experience. They were able to see and describe nature in the round.

When *The Hebrides* was in its early stages of production Morton's time was taken up with his final years as the Director (Scotland) of the Nature Conservancy

Council and then, in the later stages, by the need to
conserve his energies because of an illness. Through this
period he needed an assistant to help with the compilation, primary drafting and editing of his text, the incor-
poration of expert comment and the application of the
judgement and taste of a younger scientist. Morton did
not require to look further than his second son, Ian
Lamont Boyd. Ian made his first visit to the Hebrides in
infancy, and came face to face with a grey seal, the
animal which was eventually to be the subject of his
Cambridge PhD dissertation, for the first time at the age
of 19 months. Throughout his boyhood he was continuously on foot with his father in the Hebrides and later,
like Morton, had the benefit of a broadly-based Degree in
natural science from a Scottish University. Ian has pur-
sued a career in scientific research and is now in charge of
seal research at the British Antarctic Survey.

Both hardback and softback editions of *The Hebrides*
went out of print within 18 months of publication in
1990. HarperCollins decided not to reprint, but made the
book available to Birlinn for reprinting in three shorter
books. The authors, therefore, have restructured *The
Hebrides* and have provided new Prefaces, Chapters,
Bibliographies and Indexes for all three new books. The
chapters of the original book have been reprinted
with a few amendments; it has not been possible, on
account of cost, to update the text of 1990.

The authors were faced with a vast span in geological
age, an enormous number of distinct forms of life all of
which are specially adapted to their living quarters, a
wide range of temperate maritime habitats and a group of
human influences and impacts on the environment rooted
in Celtic and Norse cultures, and strikingly different
today from those in mainland Britain. The whole great
assembly is dynamic. It is not sufficient, therefore, to
provide a snap-shot of nature and human affairs today:
one also has to apply the dimension of history and unrelenting change. To achieve this in three short volumes it
was a matter of, firstly, choosing how much to include of
the available knowledge; secondly, consulting with special-
ists with knowledge about the subject of each chapter;
and thirdly, incorporating these experts' comments.

The authors are deeply aware that the shape and content of this book and its two companions are a matter of
personal choice. It has been difficult to decide what
should be excluded; there are many studies which deserve
mention and which, in the hands of other compilers,

would find a place. The fact that some works are restricted to a mention in the Bibliography does not necessarily reflect their importance in natural and human history. The authors thank the following who have provided valuable unpublished information and other special advice in the writing of this book and its two companion volumes: R. N. Campbell for the distribution lists of brackish-freshwater fishes, amphibians, reptiles and mammals in Appendix 4; A. Currie and Mrs C. Murray for revising their list of vascular plants; the Department of Biological Sciences, University of Stirling for a copy of *Mariculture Report 1988*; Professor P. A. Jewell for data on Soay sheep at St Kilda; Scottish Natural Heritage for a copy of *Agriculture & Environment in the Outer Hebrides* and, together with the Seabird Group, for data from the Seabird Colony Register; Dr M. A. Ogilvie and Dr D. A. Stroud for data on wintering geese; Miss M. G. Roy for helpfully abstracting climatic data from *Scotland's Climate* (Meteorological Office, 1988). Advice on Gaelic literature and names of flora, fauna, rocks and minerals has been given by Alan M. Boyd.

The authors also thank the authors of papers in the two volumes in the *Proceedings of the Royal Society of Edinburgh* (1979, 1983) which were a rich source of material for these books and A. R. Waterston (1981) without whose efforts the natural history of the Hebrides would remain scattered and inaccessible. We also thank the following for advice and practical help; K. J. Boyd, R. D. Cramond, Miss A. Coupe, Mrs H. G. Foster, Sir Charles A. Fraser, R. Goodier, F. Hamilton, Mrs S. Scott, Prof. A. D. McIntyre, Dr D. S. McLusky, Dr D. H. Mills, Dr H. Prendergast, and others.

Over almost forty years, many naturalists who have not been directly involved in the writing of this book, have shared with Morton their knowledge of the Hebrides. The authors have in mind colleagues in the Nature Conservancy (1957–73) and Nature Conservancy Council (1973–85)—especially J. C. (later The Viscount of) Arbuthnott, M. E. Ball, R. N. Campbell, A. Currie, Dr W. J. Eggeling, Dr D. A. Ratcliffe, J. G. Roger, and P. Wormell; the members of the Soay Sheep research Team at St Kilda (1959–67)—especially Prof. P. A. Jewell and Dr C. Milner; the Grey Seal Research Programme at North Rona and Harris (1959–69)—especially R. Balharry, R. H. Dennis and J. MacGeoch; the Rum National Nature Reserve (1965–85)—especially Dr T. H. Clutton-Brock and Miss F. E. Guinness; and the Sea

Eagle   Reintroduction   Project   (1975–85)—especially
R. H. Dennis, J. A. Love and H. Misund. We wish to
take this opportunity of thanking them and saluting them
for their knowledge of natural science and their contribution to the conservation of nature in the Hebrides.

The typescripts and proofs were corrected by Mrs
W. I. Boyd, Mrs S. M. E. Boyd and R. D. Cramond.
The authors also wish to thank the following who kindly
read and commented on one or more chapters of this
book and its two companion volumes—an asterisk
denotes more than one chapter. Miss. S. S. Anderson,
R. S. Bailey, M. E. Ball★, Prof. R. J. Berry★, Dr J. L.
Campbell, R. N. Campbell★. Dr T. H. Clutton-Brock,
R. D. Cramond★, A. Currie★, Dr D. J. Ellett, Dr C. H.
Emeleus★. Dr P. G. H. Evans, Dr R. J. Harding, Dr
M. P. Harris, Dr G. Hudson, Prof. P. A. Jewell, G. S.
Johnstone, R. C. B. Johnstone, A. J. Kerr, J. Lindsay, Dr
R. A. Lindsay, J. A. Love, Prof. A. D. McIntyre, H.
McLean, Dr D. S. McLusky, Dr P. S. Maitland★, Dr J.
Mason, Dr A. Mowle, S. Murray, Prof. T. A. Norton,
Dr M. A. Ogilvie, Dr R. E. Randall, Prof. W. Ritchie,
Miss M. G. Roy, Dr D. A. Stroud★, Dr D. J. Smith, Dr
M. L. Tasker★, Miss V. M. Thom, Dr P. J. Tilbrook,
A. R. Waterston, Dr C. D. Waterston, Dr R. C. Welch,
and P. Wormell★.

J. Morton Boyd
and Ian L. Boyd
Balephuil
Isle of Tiree
Argyll

Prologue—
Islands on the Edge

CHAPTER I

*The Hebrideans were an entity to me, as an extraordinary
amalgam of hard-bitten practicality and high spiritual indiffer-
ence to commercial prosperity and I knew their folklore. There
was also a regard for the creatures of land and sea, completely
unsentimental, and yet accepting an identity with the whole
environment which reminded me of the Columban Christian
association of people with those other denizens of land and sea.
The Hebridean gathered a store of young gannets for winter
food and killed seals for sea boots and oil, but he did not kill
for fun.*

*But that was yesterday and far beyond, into a prehistory
when Pytheas circumnavigated the islands of Northern Britain,
when some Mediterranean folk had already raised the Callernish
Circle of great stones and set the fact of human occupation.
Yesterday when we were young, the natural resources of land
and sea were, with the six-rowed bere, the bread grain, the
staff of life, but history had upset any golden age in our
imagination. The Vikings had been and some had stayed,
adopting the Gaelic as their tongue but making over two-thirds
of the place names Scandinavian. Gael and Mediterranean were
so much themselves that the physical type persists today almost
as a genetic segregate; the first question to a midwife was often
as to whether the baby was a 'Spaneach' or not. The folk had
culturally become one and the wild resources of the land and sea
supported them. Even North Rona, when visited by Martin
Martin in the 17th century, had its 30 people, paying their
proper respect to the environment in their own religious way.
But the 18th century was an era of development—the sacred
word which we are even now scarcely questioning . . .*

*Conservation applied to care through wise use, is a word
which originated in America in the first years of this century. It
came into the open at the White House Conference in 1908*
(and is today continued in the popular cant phrase of
'sustainable development'). *Great Britain was remarkably
unheeding, although so devoted, uncritically, to the protection of
wild animals. The basic necessity of maintaining an ecologically
complete habitat seems scarcely to have been comprehended. Nor*

has it yet in many walks of life. But the Hebridean hates waste as a sin. His or her wealth of cultural background does not waste wildlife either.

Island life needs special gifts which the environment can develop. One is living near the edge so that, like the Eskimo, a multiplicity of physical possessions can be an embarrassment. Riches can accumulate in social achievement. Language as a means of communication, the arts of music and poetry, are part of the cultural heritage which radio (TV, video), and sound recording can enrich—and they can impoverish.

These lines were among the last written by Sir Frank Fraser Darling before his death in 1979, and describe in a nutshell what this book is about. The time has long since passed for self-sufficiency in community life throughout the developed world. Even the most remote previously self-reliant peoples, like those in the highlands of Papua New Guinea, are now being rapidly opened up to monetary culture and exploitive development. The barter economy and spirit of self-help, which has made island life so attractive to the outsider since Dr Johnson's time, still persists in crofting townships, but can no longer be considered a bondage for community. Most families do not have the wherewithal in kind and manpower for traditional reciprocity and are greatly dependent on a variety of Government and European subsidies.

Rehabilitation schemes for agriculture, fishing and cottage industries have not succeeded in reversing the decline in all of these employments. Fish farming and tourism have been the 'sunrise' industries in the Hebrides in concert with the rest of Britain. The construction and operation of the Guided Weapons Range in the southern Outer Hebrides has played a great part in raising the economies of Benbecula and the Uists. The future of such prosperity is as precarious as the future of the Range itself, in the defence strategy of the North Atlantic Treaty Organisation. The people have a limited say as to what their future will be.

The latest proposed development is the creation of a superquarry at Lingerabay in Harris. The anorthosite, and other related rocks of Roineabhail, are highly sought after as a pale roadstone. Big business has a plan to pave many future motorways with this rock, shipped direct from Harris to distant ports. A great controversy has arisen over the proposals and the Scottish Secretary has instituted a public enquiry to advise him on the decision on whether to allow the development.

The anorthosite was elaborated in the earth's crust over 1,500 million years ago, when the crustal plate, of which the Highlands and Islands of Scotland and Northern Ireland are a part, was placed in equatorial latitudes. Over this enormous span of time, through unimaginable epochs of crustal movement, metamorphosis, sedimentation and erosion, the ancient rocks are now placed in north-west Scotland exposed to the atmosphere. In its entirety, the basement of the Hebridean Shelf has a heritage deeper in time than any other part of the British Isles. Has this rock of the ages been created for the sole purpose of use and virtual destruction by man, a creature of a mere two million years? Any theory of convergent predestiny of the anorthosite and the quarrymasters beggars belief, and smacks of a crass, cavalier human disrespect for the inscrutable might and mystery of nature.

The natural capital is not only accounted for in rock; it is also vested in the natural beauty of scenery, the natural-ness of the unpolluted Outer Hebrides and tranquillity in a country where peace and quietness is in short supply. The short-term advantages to a small number of local employees will be off-set by the distribution of profits elsewhere, and the spoliation of an undisturbed environ-ment, cherished by on-coming generations of residents and visitors alike. A huge scar engraved upon the face of Harris would be an eye-sore visible on a clear day for 50 miles, and an enduring monument to the folly of its creators.

Let not Lingerabay be yet another exploitive episode in the history of the Highlands and Islands, which have seen

The orca or killer whale is a predator of seals, porpoises and dolphins and hunt among the Hebrides May to October—a large bull (Photo: I. L. Boyd)

their resources of people and nature abused and abandoned over centuries. Let this, at last, be an age of enlightenment which sees the end of spoliation of wild country, and an embrace of the civilising effects which it has upon the lives of its people. Lingerabay may have its momentary benefits, but it will not make the Hebrides a happier and more habitable land.

I have seen the orca hunting off the dun,
a little chapel buried in the sands
and a headstone to seven sibs, victims of disease.
I have seen the fortitude of men tested in the gales
and time marked upon the land as dykes, sheilings and quays
where silver fish once slipped between hard hands,
and where perished dreams of better times
amongst the Hebrides.

Also the notion of scent and mire
is a little scaled within our fire
of peat-block blazing in the grate
below the thatch, while rivers spate.
Where once the polished panels shone
reflecting the firelight and the chime
of ancient song;
the rhyme of mouth and ear was handed down
the generations strong.
Now, the shine has gone, hard walls crumble;
in old lades the spearworts bloom
and nettles cover the kiln's cold hearth.
The croft door lies ajar
unlocked and ever open to the wind,
for death has brought another lineage in.

Iris flags and the Eleocharis, rush the inbye land
shrouding a half-bottle thrown in the pain
and hopeless trough of burdened life;
and at a past so quaint and lush.
But hark! That laughter of a child
begins a new and tempting fate to see
where, among the tangles from the sea,
we begin, once more, to 'hold the Hebrides.

Flitting on the wave far off, the brilliant colours of the sails
complete a scene so full of energy and joy,
where hearts beat fast around the buoy.
The burnet moths or corncrakes on the overlooking hill
take flight once more before the setting moon
threatens darkness on a precious land.
Let's hope the rose-root blooms once more
and the petrels skim the clean-foamed tops
of waves crooned from the deep sea swells.
Between the islands a channel flows
where a small boat tacks to Hough
bringing in and sewing again,
the creels which reap the sea so thin.

Back and forth the ferries ply
bringing strangers to their new-found seats,
while vain promise seeks to swell those new heart beats.
These vernal tints, like the primrose, bloom
stark amongst the withered past which prevail
only to be faded like the rainbow's veil.
And through all this there stands serene
a frieze of orchids, mountains and seas;
the orca and the Land—beloved Hebrides!

I. L. Boyd

CHAPTER 2 **Profile of an Archipelago**

The Written Record

The Western Isles of Scotland which make the subject of this book, were called by the ancient geographers Aebudae and Hebrides; but they knew little of them, that they neither agreed in their name nor number. Perhaps it is peculiar to those isles that they have never been described until now by any man that was a native of the country or had travelled them. They were indeed touched by Boethius, Bishop Lesly, Buchanan and Johnstone, in their histories of Scotland; but none of those authors were ever there in person: so that what they wrote concerning them was upon the trust of others. Buchanan, it is true, had his information from Donald Monro, who had been in many of them; and therefore his account is the best that has hitherto appeared, but it must be owned that it is very imperfect: the great man designed the history, and not the geography of his country, and therefore in him is pardonable. Besides since his time there is a great change in the humour of the world, and by consequence in the way of writing. Natural and experimental philosophy has been much improved since his days; and therefore descriptions of countries without the natural history of them, are now justly reckoned to be defective . . .

Thus Martin Martin began *A Description of the Western Isles of Scotland* (1703) in a condescending tone to the then only existing first hand account of the islands by Donald Monro, High Dean of the Isles *c.* 1549 (first published in 1774). Martin's own efforts are now dwarfed by the great body of knowledge which has accrued to the present day; nonetheless his account, and that of Monro, stands today as the invaluable datum of Hebridean history. Everything before Monro is prehistory, though research in the Scottish and Irish archive may yet bring to light a medieval account of the Hebrides so far unknown. In the 18th and 19th centuries, Pennant's *Voyage* (1774–76), MacCulloch's *Description* (1819 and 1824), Macgillivray's *Account* (1930) all added greatly to knowledge of the flora, fauna, and rocks of the Hebrides. The compilers of *Statistical Accounts* of 1791–99, and 1845 added much flesh to the bones of previous works, giving a view not only of the country but of the utilisation of natural resources, and the customs of the people. Hugh Miller in *The Cruise of the Betsey* (1869) and Harvie-Brown, firstly with Buckley (1888 and 1892), and secondly with Macpherson (1904) in the three *Vertebrate Faunas* made signal contributions to the natural history of the Hebrides, the neighbouring mainland in Argyll and the North-West Highlands. These books were written by amateur naturalists possessing the spirit of scholarship, exploration and discovery which marked the decades following publication of the *Origin of Species* (1859).

In the Darwinian period, the publication by the Ordnance Survey of the first editions of the 1:63,360 and the 1:10,560 series in 1876 gave the modern geographical base to the archipelago, and enormous impetus to survey work. There followed the Geological Survey under Geikie and others, and the Bathymetrical Survey of the freshwater lochs by Murray and Pullar (1910) and, much later, the Soil Survey by the Macaulay Institute (1947), the West Highland Survey by Fraser Darling and others (1944–49), and many specialised surveys in the past forty years reviewed by Morton Boyd and others in *The Natural Environment of the Hebrides* (*Outer* 1979; *Inner* 1983). There has been a census of the human population each decade commencing in 1801, with one previous in 1755, and none in 1941. In 1755 the total for the Hebrides was 41,670; the maximum was 93,350 in 1841; in 1991 there were 47,218. The population curve is bell-shaped showing a steady increase to 1841, and thereafter a decrease, except 1871–1901 when it was fairly steady about 79,000.

In the preface to his account of the geological structure of the Western Isles, MacCulloch (1819) remarks on the struggle he had to exclude a great amount of repetitive detail in his description of the islands; yet he hardly scratched the surface of our present knowledge, for his successors have served to put a level of detail on record such that there is hardly a corner of these islands or an aspect of their history, culture, and science which has not been explored and described. A glance at the bibliography of *The Hebrides* (Boyd and Boyd, 1990) shows the scale in which the archipelago has been described, particularly in the past half century. Monographs of varying scholarship have been written on many of the islands, and those by John Lorne Campbell on Canna (1984), and Mairi McArthur on Iona (1990) are classics. A recent bibliography of St Kilda (Quine, 1982) carries the titles of 72 books, and a further 72 papers and articles. Nonetheless, the Hebrides still withhold their secrets from even the most devoted scholar and explorer; in their ever changing faces, the islands bear forward the imprint of evolution of nature and people into the future.

Geographical Outline

The Hebrides lie between the latitudes 55°34′N at the Mull of Oa, Islay and 59°10′N at North Rona, and between longitudes 05°44′W at Kyle Rhea, Skye and 08°03′W at St Kilda. The archipelago is 385 km (241 miles) from north to south, and 189 km (118 miles) from east to west. History and geography have divided the archipelago into the Inner and Outer Hebrides separated by the 22-km strait of the Little Minch. To the west the islands face the open Atlantic ocean; to the east they face the western seaboard of mainland Scotland, from which they are separated by tidal channels of 20 m at Clachan, Seil, Argyll and 300 m at Kyle Rhea, Skye. The coastline is probably in excess of 4,000 km (2,500 miles) in length; Skye alone has a coastline of c. 460 km (288 miles).

There are 270 (151 *Inner*, 119 *Outer*) named islands in the 1:250,000 map of the Hebrides, all but a few of which are used for agriculture, mainly as grazings for sheep and cattle. Only 41 (27 *Inner*, 14 *Outer*) are permanently inhabited: *Inner*—Skye, Raasay, Scalpay (Skye), Pabay, Soay, Canna, Sanday, Rum, Eigg, Muck, Coll, Tiree, Mull, Ulva, Iona, Inchkenneth, Eraid, Lismore, Kerrera, Seil, Luing, Shuna, Jura, Colonsay, Oronsay, Islay and Gigha; *Outer*—Lewis, Harris, Great Bernera, Scalpay (Harris), Berneray (Harris), North Uist, Grimsay, Baleshare, Benbecula, South Uist, Eriskay, Barra, Vatersay and Hirta (Army garrison). The land area, 0.69 million hectares (1.7 million acres), includes extensive areas of tidal flat flooded at times of high spring tides, and freshwater lochs (*Inner* 0.40 million ha, *Outer* 0.29 million ha) (Murray, 1973). There are over 7,580 lochs shown on the 1:63,360 OS maps of the Hebrides (*Inner* 1,542, *Outer* 6,038 including 4,136 in Lewis and Harris). The largest loch is Langavat in Lewis, 8.9 sq. km, but the vast majority are less than 0.25 sq. km. There are 2,990 streams entering the sea (*Inner* 1,615; *Outer* 1,375), but 2,632 (88%) are minor, and only 5 (0.2%) are major streams, three in Lewis and Harris, and one each in Skye

and Mull (Maitland and Holden, 1983; Waterston *et al.*, 1979).

The scenery is of an undulating shelf. The islands are the uplifted platforms of an ancient rocky basement which is, for the most part, drowned under the Atlantic Ocean, the Minches and the Sea of the Hebrides. Into the ancient basement, great masses of younger igneous rocks were thrust at intervals, and the country was further uplifted. Throughout this vast span of geological time the country was eroding under the pressure of weather, sea and ice. Erosion and sedimentation has fashioned the scenery in which the ancient basement still persists in the Outer Hebrides, south-east Skye, Rum, Coll, Tiree, Iona, Colonsay and parts of Islay, with mountains of granite and gneiss in Harris and South Uist respectively, while the younger igneous rocks form the mountains of Skye, Rum, Mull and the islands of St Kilda. The Paps of Jura are of Cambrian quartzite and belong to rocks lying to the east of the Great Glen Fault. The islands are clad in peat, but on the west coast of the outer islands from the Rhinns of Islay to the Butt of Lewis there are major drifts of marine sand which have ameliorated the peaty coastal plains and provided a basis for agriculture. Otherwise the islands are bare and barren, and bereft of woodland except on the sheltered sides of the inner islands, and certain selected sheltered localities on the leeward coast of the outer islands, notably at Stornoway and Colonsay.

There are three outstanding landscapes which mark the different geologies of the Hebrides. The *machair* or sea meadow is a complex of arcuate beaches of shell sand backed by sand dunes and plains of flowery meadows

Machair in bloom with daisies, buttercups and clovers at Balinoe, Tiree (Photo: J. M. Boyd)

(machair) with shallow lagoon-like lochs bordering the rocky, undulating hinterland of the islands. The *cuillins* of Skye and Rum, beloved of mountaineers, are the roots of ancient volcanoes which rise through the Archaean basement to form dramatic mountain skylines. In Skye there are broadly two rock types—the gabbros form the serrated peaks of the Black Cuillin, and the granites form the elegant paps of the Red Cuillin. The same comparison can be made between the gabbros and the granites at St Kilda. Finally, the *columnar basalts* are the lava plateaux of the Inner Hebrides culminating in the Sgurr of Eigg and Staffa with Fingal's Cave, and providing the stepped landscapes in Mull, Treshnish Isles, Eigg, Canna, north Skye (MacLeod's Tables, The Storr, Quiraing), Raasay and the Shiant Isles.

At the 1971 census the population of the Hebrides was 61,209: *Inner*—15,371 (Skye 7,481, Islay 3,875, Mull 2,170 and less than 1,000 in all others); *Outer*—45,838 (Lewis 20,739 including Stornoway 5,279, Harris 2,963, North Uist 1,807, Benbecula and South Uist 3,799, and Barra 1,159 and less than 1,000 in all others). A large proportion of the population is dispersed throughout the islands in crofting townships and farms. The main centres of population are in the Burgh of Stornoway in Lewis, in the small towns of Portree and Broadford in Skye, Port Ellen, Port Charlotte and Bowmore in Islay, Tobermory in Mull, Castlebay in Barra, Balivanich in Benbecula, Leverburgh in Harris and many villages of which

Tobermory, Mull showing the waterfront buildings on the raised beach with a perched sea-cliff behind them, and the upper village on the cliff top (Photo: J. M. Boyd)

Kyleakin, Port Askaig, Scalasaig, Craignure, Scarinish, Arinagour, Lochboisdale, Lochmaddy, and Tarbert are important in the infrastructure of the archipelago, with mainland ferry connections to Kintyre, Oban, Mallaig, Uig and Ullapool. Causeways connect North Uist, Benbecula and South Uist, and another connects Vatersay and Barra. Bridges connect Lewis with Great Bernera, Canna with Sanday and Seil with the mainland, and a large bridge is now under construction connecting Skye with the mainland. Local ferries connect Islay with Jura; Skye with the Small Isles, Raasay, and the mainland; Mull with Iona, Morven and Ardnamurchan; South Uist with Eriskay and Barra; North Uist with Bernera and Harris. Main air services are from Glasgow and Inverness to airports in Islay, Tiree, Barra, Benbecula and Stornoway and there are emergency landing strips and helipads in Oronsay, Mull, Coll, Harris and Skye.

The main industries are agriculture, fishing, fish farming and tourism. Agriculture and fishing have been the employment of the Gael since time immemorial. The hunter-fisher people of the 5th millenium BC probably preceded the stone-age farmers by a thousand years, and since then the islands have been pastured and the seas and freshwaters fished. Fish farming and tourism, on the other hand, are employments of the last few decades of this century, and will be looked upon by future historians as belonging to the 3rd millenium AD.

Hebridean agriculture, in concert with trends in Britain and Europe, has undergone a transformation from a mixed economy of livestock, grass, cereal and root-crop production, to a grass intensive economy focused on subsidised livestock farming. Accent has been placed on the reclamation of peat moorland to green pasture, and the improvement of lowland pastures by drainage, fertilising and reseeding. The area of crops has decreased dramatically not only because of economic factors, but also due to the ageing of the crofting and farming population, the part-time nature of crofting, difficulties in livestock marketing in remote areas, and the lack of suitable machinery and seeds for small-holding agriculture.

Gone are the days of the prolific Hebridean sea fishery to which the economic prosperity of the Outer Hebrides has been keyed. All sections of the community, from the owners of modern vessels to the local short-line fishermen in open boats, have been affected by the decline in fish stocks. Herring spawning grounds occur west and north of Lewis, and larvae drift eastward to nursery areas.

Enhanced recruitment in the late 1960s, and an increase in fishing effort with the use of 'pair trawl' and 'purse seine' nets produced a large, but short-lived, increase in landings. The harvesting of the stocks of herring, mackerel, sprats, sand eels and Norway pout for fish meal and other industrial purposes, against a background of unpredicted natural fluctuations, has greatly reduced the pelagic fishery. This has resulted in the introduction of quotas, and the laying up of many vessels.

The demersal fishery is based mainly on haddock, whiting and cod mostly from spawning grounds on the Hebridean shelf, with some recruitment from the North Sea. In the course of this century, the trawling industry has scarified the Hebridean shelf, and extinguished what was a wonderfully rich renewable natural resource. The greed of the trawl owners to take all and leave nothing for posterity has contributed to the near destruction of once abundant fish stocks taken beyond their thresholds of regeneration. Local inshore men were summarily deprived of a livelihood, and communities of food. The same can be said for the purse seiners with equipment by which they can relentlessly pursue and scoop entire shoals of pelagic fish, leaving none for wildlife nor future people. The lobstermen, prawners, scallop dredgers and velvet crabbers also take all they can get, with many boats working the same grounds to the point of exhaustion. Fishermen have a hard life, but it has been made much harder today by the greed of the fishermen of

The Caledonian-McBrayne Kyleakin–Kyle of Lochalsh ferry Loch Fyne *in the last week of its life, just previous to opening of the Skye Bridge in October 1995 (Photo: J. M. Boyd)*

yesterday. Do the fishermen of today have regard for the fishermen of tomorrow?

Fish farming has grown from nothing in the 1960s to a major industry in the Highlands and Islands. The Hebrides have had their share of development. By 1990 there were 87 fish farms in the Hebrides (*Inner* 28; *Outer* 59) producing salmon, trout, and marine shellfish, with a further 20 in development. The Hebrides provide near ideal sites for fish farming with plenty of clean fresh water close to the shore for the tanks in the first stages, and clean, continuously exchanging sea water for the cages in the second stage of growth of the fish. Shellfish, which are reared on natural food, require a continuous movement of plankton-rich sea water. Shelter is also important. Such conditions are found in Loch Roag and the eastern seaboard of the Outer Hebrides, and in the sheltered kyles and sea lochs of Skye. The industry has provided employment in remote areas and has become a major quantum of prosperity in the Outer Hebrides and Skye. On the down side, fish farms can be unsightly in areas of fine scenery and, if poorly managed, can have a significant impact on wildlife: the seabed beneath the cages can become foul with food waste and faeces; damage by seals, otters, herons, cormorants and eiders is likely in the Hebrides, and local populations of these protected species may be adversely affected; escaped farmed salmon may pose a threat to the genotype of wild salmon breeding in Scottish rivers; chemicals and anti-biotics for control of fouling, disease and infestations of the salmon louse kill other non-parasitic species, including lobster larvae (Nature Conservancy Council, 1989).

As long ago as 1773 Dr Samuel Johnson was attracted to the Hebrides. He was perhaps the first tourist to leave a record of his journey. He started a fashion which has continued ever since. The coming of the steam engine on rail and sea last century made the Hebrides accessible to an urban, industrial society in need of escape from drudgery and smog. This was followed by the advent of the motor car, coach, ferry and aircraft which, since the end of the Second World War, have transformed the remote character of the Highlands and Islands. Thus was born the tourist industry which flourishes today as a major industry trading on the cultural and natural qualities of the islands. The exoticism of the Hebrides, which has appealed for two centuries to the British people, is now running in the veins of continental Europeans, who find an 'oceanic' environment and people in the Hebrides, the like of which is unknown in their home land. From North America and Australia come the descendants of those who left the islands seeking new lives in the colonies. On the wave of nostalgia they seek their forebears and the sites of homesteads of long ago. Many people from the mainland have second homes in the islands, and there are major attractions: wildlife, walking, climbing, painting and cultural holidays; angling for salmon, trout and sea fish; sailing and wind-surfing.

Geology and Soils

The rocks of the Outer Hebrides and the Inner Hebrides are very different. The former is an eroded platform of Lewisian gneiss, a rock which was already in existence 3 billion years ago. The latter is a highly diversified platform containing fragments of the Lewisian gneiss with its associated Torridonian sandstone, limestones and sandstones of a great Jurassic estuary, and large spreads of Tertiary volcanic rocks. During this span of time there have been many geological episodes, and the Palaeozoic and Mesozoic rocks have been transferred by crustal movement from latitudes south of the equator to their present temperate latitudes. The first episode, between 2.8 and 1.6 billion years ago, was the emplacement within the gneiss of the mass of granite now occupying North Harris and South Lewis. This granite has on its southern boundary an equally old complex of epidiorites and schists which traverse the southern part of South Harris and the western half of Taransay. This complex contains the anorthosite of Lingerabay which is the site of a proposed superquarry. Other small outcrops of schist occur in north Lewis, and in the Uists. The Mesozoic and Tertiary rocks which are so well represented in the Inner Hebrides are restricted in the Outer Hebrides. The only sedimentary rocks, possibly of Triassic age, occur around Stornoway where sandstones and conglomerates form the isthmus of the Eye Peninsula and the western coast of Broad Bay. St Kilda and the Shiant Isles have Tertiary rocks.

The Great Estuarine Series consists of interbedded Triassic, Jurassic and Cretaceous sandstones and limestones which have been interrupted by, and buried under, Tertiary volcanic rocks in Skye, Raasay, Eigg and Mull. The rocks are in places richly fossiliferous, and show that the estuary was probably tropical or sub-tropical in climate.

The Tertiary volcanic centres are situated in Mull, Ardnamurchan, Rum, Skye and St Kilda. These were Eocene volcanoes of about 60 million years ago, and all that now remains of them are their roots and some of the lava fields which they created. The Cuillins of Skye and Rum, the hills of Mull and the whole of the St Kilda group are the magma chambers of volcanoes the ash and lava piles of which have long since been eroded away. The plateau basalts of Muck, Eigg, Canna, north Skye and Raasay are what remains of the lava floods and the torrential rains of cinder, ash and dust which came from them over a period of millions of years. During the life of these volcanoes, enormous earthquakes with centres in Skye and Mull resulted in dense swarms of dolerite dykes transecting the country rocks from north-west to south-east. The alignment of dykes in Colonsay, Jura, Islay and Gigha is towards the volcanic centre in Arran which was contemporaneous with those in the Hebrides.

The geology of the north-west of Scotland contains five major faults running from north-east to south-west. These form the boundaries of different crustal masses which became attached during tectonic movements across the earth's surface in the immense span of geological time. The Great Glen Fault runs from Shetland to Ireland and passes through the Firth of Lorne, separating Lismore from Kingairloch, clipping the south-east tip of Mull, and passing just north of Colonsay to the coast of Ireland. The Moine Thrust emerges from the sea at Loch Eriboll in Sutherland, and runs south through the North-West Highlands, passing through Sleat in Skye, probably clipping the eastern tip of Rum, passing through the Sound of Iona and running on southward into the ocean bed. The Camasunary-Skerryvore Fault runs through the Rum and Tiree Passages from Loch Scavaig in Skye to Skerryvore. The Minch Fault runs through the beds of the Minch, the Little Minch and the Sea of the Hebrides all of which have deep trenches in the gneiss basement. Through the ages, these trenches have become filled with much younger sedimentaries, to which the sandstones of Lewis may be related. Finally, there is the Outer Hebrides Thrust which follows the eastern coast of the Outer Hebrides and forms the eastern boundary of the Lewisian platform.

The Hebrides are part of the continental margin fragmented by the parting of the European and North American crustal plates. Later this margin was glaciated, with the development of westward thrusting glaciers trenching the Caledonian plateau. During the recession of the last (Quaternary) ice sheet about 10,000 years ago, late glacial centres with ice-caps and glaciers persisted in Harris, Skye, Rum, Mull, Jura and Islay. The recession and advance of Quaternary ice resulted in changes in sea-level with raised beaches and, in the mountains, cliffs and scree slopes (Sissons, 1965).

The resulting landforms are varied, and controlled by the nature of the rocks. The ancient granites of Harris, the Tertiary volcanic centres in Skye, Rum and Mull and the quartzites of Jura, are mountainous with high ridges interspaced with glaciated valleys and rock basins. The black Cuillins of Skye and Rum have peaks and serrated ridges of gabbro which contrast with the smooth rounded granite hills of Harris, the Red Cuillin of Skye, the quartzites of Jura and the broad-backed basalt hills in parts of Mull, Jura and Islay. The Tertiary lava plateaux in north Skye, Canna, Sanday, Eigg, Mull and the Treshnish Isles have angular, stepped landscapes with table land and scarps culminating in An Sgurr in Eigg, and often possessing spectacular columnar jointing so wonderfully displayed at Fingal's Cave on Staffa, and the Kilt Rock at Staffin on Skye. Islands with gneisses and Torridonian sandstone have also gently terraced country with freakish coastal features. These occur in the sandstone in north Rum and Colonsay, and undulating terrain of low hills and hollows with uneven low cliffs and scree slopes in the gneiss of south-east Skye, Coll, Tiree, Iona and west Islay. The quartzites of Scarba, north Jura, east Islay and Gigha also provide broken country with alignments of ridges and valleys, reflecting the strike of the rocks and the direction of glaciation.

The soils closely reflect the geology. Broadly, the soils which are derived from the gneisses, Torridonian sandstone and the granites are acid and infertile in character, compared with those derived from the basalts, gabbros and ultra basic rocks which yield fertile soils. Those soils which come from the erosion of the country rock are modified by the accretion of calcareous shell sand taken from solution in the sea by marine organisms. The parent materials are in: *glacial tills* found as the scour of Tertiary weathering, and a precipitate from Pleistocene ice moving across the Lewisian platform of the Outer Hebrides, the quartzites of Jura and the basalts and Jurassic shales of Skye; *morainic drift* deposited by glaciers in the valleys of all the mountainous islands and which are usually more permeable than tills; *outwash fan* and *raised beach* consisting

The Kilt Rock,
Trotternish, Skye with
the waterfall from Loch
Mealt. A near
horizontal sill of
columnar olivine
dolerite (resembling
pleats) overlies Jurassic
sediments in a 60 m sea
cliff (Photo: J. M.
Boyd)

of rounded water-worn particles and pebbles, created by
the downwash of gravels and sands by streams into
valleys and sea, and by the uplift of the land following
the disappearance of the ice sheet in the last 10,000 years;
colluvium as the product of breakdown of bare rock by
weathering, and gravitating to fill hollows in the knock-
and-lochan country such as in the Uists, the Ross of
Mull, eastern Jura and Trotternish, Skye; *aeolian sand*
occurring in great drifts on the western coasts of the
outer islands from Islay to Lewis with spectacular dune
systems in Tiree, Coll, Barra, Monach Islands and
Luskentyre in Harris; and *montane detritus* created by the
freeze-thaw cycle on the upper reaches of the mountains
giving rise to scree and fjellfields.

Almost half of the land surface of the main islands is
masked by deep peat, which overlies all types of rock.
Anaerobic waterlogged conditions are widespread, and
override the mineral character of the rock and soil base.
Under the peat, peaty podsols, humus-iron podsols, peaty
gleys and non-calcereous gleys occur together, and vary
according to mineral content, topography and drainage.
These are the soils of the glacial tills, morainic drifts and
colluvium, which dominate the interiors of the islands
clad in Atlantic heath. Brown forest soils occur over free

draining basalt and calcareous detritus on the lower
ground of glens, and often in outwash fans and raised
beach platforms. Many of these occupy the cultivated
land of crofts and farms, and merge with the calcareous
drifts of aeolian shell sand on coastal plains. The machair
soils, from dry dune to marsh habitat are regosols—
unconsolidated sandy loams without structure, and subject
to erosion. Above 400 m, subalpine podsols are dis-
tinguished from lower altitude soils by the mixing of the
mineral and humic horizons by the freeze–thaw cycle.
Above 700 m alpine podsols possess thin mixed mineral,
humus and stone layers, with periglacial stone stripes on
the surface.

Climate and Hydrography

The Hebrides have a warm moist climate greatly
influenced by temperate ocean currents. The North
Atlantic Drift, moving northward on to the Hebridean
shelf from the ocean west of Ireland, meets waters from
the Irish Sea coming from Biscay and passing through the
North Channel. North–South fronts between these two
waters lie to the west of the southern Inner Hebrides, and
to the west of the northern Outer Hebrides. In the Sea of
the Hebrides, south of Skye, there is a clockwise gyre
which takes Irish Sea water partly into the Minches and
partly round Barra Head, and northward on the west
coast of the Uists, Harris and Lewis. The climate is mild
compared with the British mainland. Mean daily temperatures near sea level in January are 5 to 5.50°C and in
July, 13.3 to 13.9°C. Annual rainfall varies from
1,020 mm (41 ins) on the low islands of Colonsay, Tiree
and Coll in the west, to 3,048 mm (122 ins) on the mountainous islands of Mull, Rum, Skye and Harris. The
rainfall for the entire archipelago in an average year is in
excess of the potential evaporation, which results in the
widespread waterlogging of soils. The average sunshine in
May is 234 hours in Tiree, and 200 in Trotternish, Skye,
but can be much less in the rain shadow of the high
islands. In the exposed islands on the western rim the
monthly average for days of winds of gale force (34
knots) and over is 5, but in January it is 12 and in June it
is 0.2 days. The high wind speeds are a major adverse
factor in tree growth and yields of crops and livestock.
    The Hebrides lie in the storm belt of the North
Atlantic and are, for most of the time, swept by frontal

depressions coursing north-westwards from mid-Atlantic to the Norwegian Sea. They are one of the windiest areas in Europe. Coming with an enormous fetch across the ocean, the winds are laden with sea salt which has a widespread ecological effect, declining from west to east. It is important to appreciate the 'feel' of the climate which cannot be adequately conveyed by statistics of temperature, wind speed and rainfall. The cooling rate on the human body of a strong damp wind with a temperature falling below about 13 °C (55 °F) increases very rapidly; to maintain the balance between normal heat production during exertion, and subsequent heat loss, requires rapid adjustment. The energy loss to plants, animals and people in the Hebridean climate can be very much greater than the mere average temperatures suggest. Cold rain driven by strong winds over periods of days is devastating to the unprotected. The 'feel' of the climate is a major factor in the promotion of the tourist industry in the Hebrides. For example, the islands provide excellent opportunities for wind surfing, but the weather is usually too cold for comfort.

The Hebrides has a high-energy weather and hydrographic system. The disadvantages of this have been sustained from time immemorial, in slow and reduced growth in terrestrial plant and animal life. In the sea, conditions of life have been much more prolific, with high biological production of vast stocks of fin fish and shell fish, and tens of thousands of hectares of shell sand drift, bringing fertility to otherwise barren islands. Shelter belts of trees have limited effect in landscapes which have long since lost their natural low-canopy, wind-clipped woodland. In the past, the enormous storm energy of the Hebrides has been largely to man's disadvantage; the colossal, enduring strength of wind, wave and tide awaits harvesting.

Flora and Fauna

The Hebrides lie on a biological frontier between continent and ocean. On the one hand, the great land mass of Eurasia stretches some 9,600 km eastward along the 57°N parallel of latitude to the shores of the Bering Sea in Kamchatka. On the other hand, the great marine pasturage of the North Atlantic stretches uninterrupted from the Sargasso Sea to the Barents Sea. The flora and fauna of the Hebrides are a statement of this unique position. In them is enshrined not only the physical beauty of plants and animals in remote places, but the profound interaction of the two great eco-systems of opposite character. From the bed of the sea to the mountain tops, the benign effect of the ocean softens the extremes of the continent and fashions the forms of behaviour of living creatures, making them, in some degree, unique to the Hebrides.

Our knowledge of the Hebridean flora and fauna can never be complete. Throughout the 19th and 20th centuries, check-lists of plants and animals of many of the main islands have been compiled. The Outer Hebrides have a biographical succinctness not possessed by the more scattered Inner Hebrides and, as a consequence, the record of the former has been greatly enhanced in recent years by four comprehensive works, *Flora* by R. J. Pankhurst and J. M. Mullin (1991), *Seaweeds* by T. A. Norton and H. T. Powell (1979), *Non-marine Invertebrate Fauna* by A. R. Waterston (1981) and *Birds* by W. A. J. Cunningham (1983). Recent reviews and bibliographies for the Inner Hebrides have been published: *Flora and Vegetation* by A. Currie and C. Murray (1983), *Birds* by T. M. Reed *et al.* (1983), *Coleoptera* by R. C. Welsh (1983) and *Lepidoptera* by P. Wormell (1983). A detailed account of the flora and fauna of the Hebrides can be found in the companion to this book *The Hebrides—a natural tapestry* by J. M. Boyd and I. L. Boyd (1996).

Flora

The most extensive plant community in the Hebrides is lowland acid heath. It is dominated by purple moor-grass, deer-grass and ling heather on the shallow peat, and accompanied, on the deep peat of the blanket mires, by cotton-grass and *Sphagnum* mosses. On the thinner peaty podsols and peaty gleys of the higher moorland, the moor-grass and deer-grass are accompanied by mat-grass and *Rhacomitrium* moss. Throughout the altitudinal range there are, in the drier areas, ling, tormentil, common violet, common milkwort, lousewort, common butterwort, heath bedstraw and creeping willow; and in the wetter areas, bog asphodel, long-leaved sundew and the lesser spearwort. The submontane grass-sedge-rush mires have purple moor-grass, carnation-grass, star sedge, soft rush and bog myrtle communities (except on Rum where bog myrtle is rare). The acid flows have yellow sedge and Sphagnum mosses; the more neutral have soft rush, common sedge and flea-sedge; and the calcareous have carnation-grass and the moss *Campylium stellatum.*

The lowland heaths on the windward coasts are transformed by wind-blown sea spray and calcareous sand, and by cultivation. During the 18th and 19th centuries great areas of hill land were tilled in *feannagan*—a form of ridge cultivation inappropriately known as 'lazybeds'— the remains of which can be seen throughout the archipelago. In the second half of the 20th century, subsidised land improvement schemes resulted in the fencing, fertilising and reseeding of moorland as cattle pasture in the Outer Hebrides, but much of this has since become rush infested.

The coastal grasslands include salt marshes, dunes, machair and the enclosed fields of crofts and farms. The salt marshes are a closely grazed sward of sea poa, red fescue, thrift, sea plantain, sea pearlwort, sea milkwort and shore orache. Cliff terraces have fescue-bent grassland with a tall herb community including sea campion, tormentil, lesser celandine, buck's horn plaintain, wild angelica, wild hyacinth, greater woodrush, the cross-leaved heath and the creeping willow. In seabird colonies, there is often rank growth of sorrel, and rocky niches possess thyme, rose-root and English stonecrop. Sand dunes are dominated by marram grass, sea sandwort, sand couch-grass, sea rocket, silverweed, lady's bedstraw, wild white clover, bird's foot trefoil, red fescue, lanceolate plantain and ragwort, with field gentian and sea centuary in the slacks. Many of these species occur on the machair plain which is dominated on well drained land by daisy,

The Grass of Parnassus (Parnassia palustris) in a wet machair community on The Reef, Tiree. Best blooms are found in the Hebrides in August (Photo: J. M. Boyd)

buttercup, hop trefoil, eyebright, yarrow, kidney vetch, heath-spotted orchid and others, and on the wet land by the cuckoo flower, ragged robin, lesser spearwort, amphibious bistort, march cinquefoil, marsh pennywort, lesser twayblade, field horsetail and the common spike rush.

The enclosed land of crofts and farms have communities of tall herbs associated with the production of hay and crops of potatoes and cereals. In the well drained areas there occur impressive stands of meadow-sweet, red-rattle, yellow-rattle, meadow rues, vetches, lesser knap-weed, corn marigold, spotted orchid, northern fen orchid and early purple orchid; and in wet areas ragged robin, cuckoo flower, yellow flag, marsh marigold, water horse-tail, lesser butterfly orchid and Grass of Parnassus. Peaty lochs have quill-wort, water-lobelia, shore weed, alternate-flowered water-milfoil, white water-lily and pond weeds; the limey lochs have stoneworts (*Chara* spp), spiked water-milfoil, the 'moss' *Fontinalis* and the pond weeds.

Natural woodlands are scarce, being restricted to gorges or clefts out of reach of grazing animals and fire. The birch-rowan-willow wood by the Abhainn a'Ghlinne in Waternish is a good example. Some small islands like Garbh Eileach in the Garvellachs, which are lightly grazed and have not been burned in recent years, have young birch woods. The total area of these natural-type woods (as distinct from planted woodlands) is probably less than 500 ha. They vary in species composition depending on soil type, drainage and exposure to wind and salt spray, with birch, sessile oak, rowan, hazel, ash, witch elm, alder, bird cherry, willows and holly in mixture. There is an assortment of communities: oak-ash-hazel; birch-oak-rowan; birch-rowan-willow; oak-ash elm-hazel. Plantations of exotic broadleaf and coniferous species, mainly sycamore, beech and spruce, have been established in the precincts of large houses, usually with a variety of decorative shrubs including the invasive *Rhododendron ponticum*. The woodlands around Lews Castle (Stornoway), Kinloch Castle (Rum), Torosay House (Mull), Colonsay House and Islay House are good examples. Commercial timber plantations have been established throughout the archipelago where soil and climatic conditions permit, using mainly Sitka and Norway spruces and lodgepole pine. In Rum, natural-type woodlands are being established using West Highland provenance Scots pine and all the native broadleaves. All these woodlands have their own field layers of grasses, tall herbs and bracken. Many of the broadleaved woods carry heavy growth of oceanic mosses, ferns, liverworts, lichens and fungi, and have a significant epiphytic fauna.

The montane communities vary with the subalpine and alpine podsols ranging from the acidic granites and quartzites in Harris and Jura, to the basic basalts of Mull and Trotternish. The acid heaths have *Rhacomitrium* moss with mat-grass, stiff sedge, creeping willow, ling, crow-berry, blaeberry, alpine club-moss, three saxifrages (purple, mossy, and snowy), Arctic mouse-ear, northern hayrattle and mountain avens. On the ultrabasic rocks there is a *Rhacomitrium* heath with Arctic sandwort, mountain rock-cress and the two-flowered rush.

Fauna

The seas of the Hebridean shelf have stocks of pelagic (surface-feeding) and demersal (bottom-feeding) fish, which have been harvested and greatly reduced in size by fishing, in the last two centuries. The pelagic species are herring, mackerel, sprat, Norway pout and sand eels. Basking sharks are also pelagic and occur in summer. The life-cycles of herring and mackerel are reasonably well researched, but those of the other pelagic species are largely unknown. It is thought that basking sharks migrate from waters off southern Ireland, following the plankton drift northward through the Hebrides and Orkney into the Norwegian Sea. They return by the way they came. Between November and February the gill rakers, with which the sharks feed, are resorbed. In winter there is little plankton on which to feed and they quit surface waters for the deeps.

The main demersal species of the fishery industry include cod, haddock, whiting, saithe, hake, spurdog, skate, plaice, lemon sole, lythe, ling, conger and angler fish. These species are widely distributed and many of them move seasonally between off-shore and on-shore grounds for spawning, nursery phases and feeding. Since time immemorial, this on-shore movement of fish has supported seasonal, local, in-shore fisheries until the second half of the 20th century, when the stocks were substantially destroyed, it is thought, by the overfishing of off-shore grounds by trawlers and seiners from distant ports. The stocks at Skerryvore and the Hawes Bank in the Sea of the Hebrides supported particularly prolific demersal fisheries, and were the rearing grounds for great concentrations of white fish which moved in-shore in late

summer to fall to the long rods of the crofter folk
perched on rocky 'carricks' on exposed headlands.

Off-shore of all islands there are also rich stocks of
shell-fish. Common and Norway lobsters, edible and
velvet crabs are the important crustaceans, but squat and
spiney lobsters and pink shrimps are common. Scallops,
queens and mussels are among the molluscs which are
harvested from the shallow seas for food, and the large
sea-urchin is also fished by skin-divers, mainly for its
decorative shell. On the sea shore there are communities
of algae and invertebrates distributed according to their
substrata, the length of time they are exposed to the air
and the force of the sea to which they are exposed.
Cockles, mussels, and periwinkles are harvested from the
shore, as were limpets in the past, their shells filling the
middens of mediaeval people. The lugworm is dug from
shore sands and used as bait for line fishing. Hebridean
shores have drifts of top shells, periwinkles and whelks.
Razor shells, and the shells of the Baltic tellin, thin tellin
and the shells and egg-case clusters of the large dog
whelk are common. Hermit crabs inhabit whelks, periwinkles and top shells. The large hermits are often in the
shells of the large dog whelk, which also bears an
anemone, a covering of encrusting algae and hydroids
and usually also houses a rag worm—a veritable micro-
cosm of marine life in the secondary use of the shell
following the death of its creator and primary occupant.

The avifauna of the Hebrides reflects well the
biogeographical character of the archipelago. The
numbers of farmland, woodland and garden birds
common in mainland Britain are uncommon, rare or
absent in the Hebrides. A comparison of the lists of
breeding birds of the National Nature Reserves of Cairn-
gorms (with Craigellachie), Rum and St Kilda illustrates
the wide differences; they have respectively 69, 54, and 25
species. Of the 69 at Cairngorm there were only two
seabirds, and of the 25 at St Kilda there were 15 seabirds.
Of the 54 on Rum, 10 were seabirds and the remainder
waders and landbirds.

As a whole, the Hebrides is one of the most important
seabird stations of the North Atlantic, possessing an array
of breeding sites for some 22 species. The largest assemblies are at St Kilda which holds about 320,000 breeding
pairs of 17 species, which is about a third of the seabirds
breeding in the Hebrides as a whole, and about a tenth of
those breeding in Britain and Ireland. The most
numerous species are puffin, fulmar, Manx shearwater,

Fulmar (Fulmarus glacialis), *the effortless flyer, is common company at sea and along the cliff edges* (Photo: I. L. Boyd)

guillemot, razorbill, kittiwake and gannet. The largest single assemblies are over 100,000 pairs of puffins and Manx shearwaters respectively at St Kilda and Rum. Other important breeding sites are Handa, Shiants, North Rona, Sulasgeir, Flannans, Mingulay, Berneray (Barra), Canna, Treshnish Isles and Colonsay.

The Hebrides receive large flocks of wintering geese from Greenland. The headquarters of the two species is in Islay where, between November and March, 27,500 barnacle geese (90% of the Greenland stock) and 5,000 Greenland white-fronted geese (25% of the Greenland stock) may use the Islay grounds. Smaller concentrations, in hundreds and tens of both species, are also found in Tiree and Coll, and barnacles only in the Treshnish, Monachs, Shiants and the islets in the Barra and Harris Sounds. Throughout the islands these Greenland species share the pasture with increasing numbers of native and migrant greylag.

The stronghold of the corncrake is in the croftlands of Tiree and the Uists where breeding has been sustained and even enhanced through the protection now offered to the species. In 1980, James Cadbury found 260 and 240 calling males respectively in the Outer and Inner Hebrides. In Tiree alone there were 85, and in 1994 there were over 110. Research has shown the habitat requirements of breeding corncrakes, and these are now being applied in the management of the hay meadows and the stands of tall herbs which are contiguous with crofter crops. Meadows are now mown from the centre outwards, giving the birds a ready escape into the tall grass and herb margins. Crofters are compensated for any loss or inconvenience which they may sustain in protecting the corncrakes on their land.

R. N. Campbell compiled data on the occurrence of

vertebrates in the Hebrides (Berry 1979 and 1983). The occurrence of freshwater fish, amphibians and reptiles are tabulated in the companion book *The Hebrides—a natural tapestry* (Boyd and Boyd, 1996), and those on mammals in the main islands, updated in 1995 by R. N. Campbell, S. Angus, A. Currie and J. A. Love, are as follows:

Species	1	2	3	4	5	6	7	8	9	10	11	12	13	14	15	16	17	18	19
Red deer	*	*		*	*	*		*	*		*					*		*	*
Fallow deer																*		E	*
Roe deer							*	*								*		*	*
Sika deer									*										
Feral goat									E	*	*			E		*	*	*	*
Feral sheep			*																
Grey seal	*	*	*	*	*	*	*	*	*	*	*	*	*	*	*	*	*	*	*
Common seal	*	*	*	*	*	*	*	*	*	*	*	*	*	*	*	*	*	*	*
Feral cat	*	*		*	*	*	*	*	*		*			*	*	*			*
Feral ferret	*	*		*	*	*			*					O		*		*	*
Weasel									*						*	*			
Stoat	?	?						*	*							*		*	*
Feral mink	*	*		*		*			E										
Otter	*	*		*	*	*	*	*	*	*	*	*	*	*	*	*	*	*	*
Badger									S										
Fox		I							*										
Brown rat	*	*		*	*	*	*	*	*	*	*	*	*	*	*	*	*	*	*
Black rat		+																	
House mouse	*	*	E	*	*	*	*	*	*	*	*	*		*	*	*	*	*	*
Field mouse	*	*	*	*	*	*	*	*	*	*	*	*	*	*	*	*	*	*	*
Water vole	*								*										*
Sht-tld vole	*	*		*	*	*			*			*	*	?	?	*		*	*
Bank vole							*		*					?	?	*		*	*
Mountain hare	*	*							*							*	*		
Brown hare	?	?		?					*						*			E	*
Rabbit	*	*		*	*	*	*	*	*		*			*	O	*	*	*	*
Pipistrelle	*	?		?	?	?		*	*	*	*	*		*		?	*	*	*
Long-eared bat									*					*		?		*	*
Daubenton's bat																	?		
Water shrew							*	*	*							*			*
Pigmy shrew	*	*		*	*	*	*	*	*	*	*	*	*	*	*	*		*	*
Common shrew	?						*	*	*			*				*		*	*
Hedgehog	*	*		*	*	*			*	*				*	*	*			*
Mole									*										
Red squirrel									I										

1 Lewis   2 Harris   3 St Kilda   4 North Uist   5 Benbecula   6 South Uist   7 Barra
8 Raasay   9 Skye   10 Canna   11 Rum   12 Eigg   13 Muck   14 Coll   15 Tiree
16 Mull   17 Colonsay   18 Jura   19 Islay

E recently extinct   *I* recently introduced   *O* domestic in captivity   *S* unconfirmed report
+confirmed report from Shiants   ? unidentified species seen.

Naturalists and Historians CHAPTER 3

16th and 17th Centuries

Donald Monro (1526–89) was the Vicar of Snizort in Skye in 1526, and Archdeacon of the Isles in 1549. His *Description of the Western Isles of Scotland* is popularly regarded as a historical datum of the Hebrides. Though it was not published until 1774, its authentic, first-hand descriptions pre-date the book by two centuries, to a time of great political and social change after the forfeiture (1493) of The Lordship and Council of the Isles by the MacDonalds for allying themselves with England. Subsequent disorder was mainly because of the weakness of the Scottish crown due to a succession of minor monarchs, and the internecine clan system thrived and endured until the Jacobite uprisings were put down by Hanoverians in 1746. Monro's *Description* is indeed sketchy, though it conveys a general impression of prosperity and mentions many items from nature.

Martin Martin MA (Edinburgh), MD (Leyden) (c. 1660–1719) was a steward and tutor in Sleat and Dunvegan, who had a perceptive and scholarly eye, and travelled widely in the Hebrides. His *Description* (1703) (p. 316) is, therefore, authentic and much more detailed than that of Monro. It begins:

... it is peculiar to those isles that they have never been described until now by any man that was a native of the country or had travelled them. They were indeed touched by Boethius, Bishop Lesly, Buchanan and Johnstone, in their histories of Scotland; but none of these authors were ever there in person ... Buchanan, it is true, had his information from Donald Monro, who had been in many of them; and therefore his account is the best that has hitherto appeared, but it must be owned that it is very imperfect: the great man designed the history, and not the geography of his country, and therefore in him is pardonable. Besides since his time there is a great change in the humour of the world, and by consequence in the way of writing. Natural and experimental philosophy has been much improved since his days; and therefore descriptions of countries, without the natural history of them, are now justly reckoned to be defective ...

A

DESCRIPTION

OF THE

𝕴𝖊𝖘𝖙𝖊𝖗𝖓 𝕴𝖘𝖑𝖆𝖓𝖉𝖘

OF

SCOTLAND.

CONTAINING

A Full Account of their Situation, Extent, Soils, Product,
Harbours, Bays, Tides, Anchoring-Places, and Fifheries.
The Antient and Modern Government, Religion and Cuftoms of
the Inhabitants ; particularly of their Druids, Heathen Temples,
Monafteries, Churches, Chappels, Antiquities, Monuments, Forts,
Caves, and other Curiofities of Art and Nature : Of their Admi-
rable and Expeditious Way of Curing moft Difeafes by Simples
of their own Product.
A Particular Account of the *Second Sight*, or Faculty of forefeeing
things to come, by way of Vifion, fo common among them.
A Brief Hint of Methods to improve Trade in that Country, both
by Sea and Land.
With a New M A P of the Whole, defcribing the Harbours, An-
choring-Places, and dangerous Rocks, for the benefit of Sailors.
To which is added, A Brief Defcription of the Ifles of *Orkney* and
Schetland.

By *M. MARTIN*, Gent.

The S E C O N D E D I T I O N, very much Corrected.

LONDON,
Printed for A. B E L L at the Crofs-Keys and Bible in *Cornhill* ;
T. V A R N A M and J. O S B O R N in *Lombard-ftreet* ; W.
T A Y L O R at the Ship, and J. B A K E R and T. W A R N E R
at the Black Boy in *Paternofter-Row.* M. DCC. XVI.

*The title page of
Martin Martin's* A
Description of the
Western Isles of
Scotland etc. *1703*

Martin's condescending treatment of earlier writings lacked
the foresight of the delayed publication of Monro's much
earlier work and of his own efforts being dwarfed by those who
were to succeed him. Nonetheless, his account and that of
Monro stand today as the beginning of the living record of the
Hebrides, in which appear vignettes of natural history from the
late 17th century. These two early accounts span the Union of
the Crowns (1603), when the Highlands and Islands were

regarded, in the words of James VI and I, as 'utterly barbarous' (Smout, 1969). Matters came to a head in 1609, when the chiefs of the Isles were surprised, captured and forced under duress to agree the Statutes of Iona. In the course of the Reformation in Scotland, these were a thrust against 'barbarism' in which the Roman Church and the Gaelic culture became casualties (Campbell, 1984). Monro saw the Isles in a much more prosperous state than Martin. Added to the social and political trauma of the Union and the Reformation, between the two *Descriptions*, there occurred the 'Little Ice Age' marked by failure of crops, poverty and destitution, all of which had a great effect on the natural environment.

Sadly, though feeling for nature is strong, for example in *Carmina Gadelica* and *The Songs of Duncan Ban Macintyre* (Macleod, 1952), there is a very small amount of natural history in Gaelic literature, indeed this aspect of native culture over centuries has gone almost unrecorded. The vital support from natural sources for human communities in food, fuel, construction and craft materials are pieced together by historians and archaeologists (Skene, 1886–90 see p. 409; Royal Commission, 1928; Mackie, 1965), but hardly mentioned by Gaelic writers. Perhaps learned orders of monks, priests and scholars did appraise their natural surroundings, and manuscripts have been lost. The romantic appeal of the scenery, flora, and fauna of the isles moved the Gaelic bards, but not usually in words of interest to the naturalist. In the Statutes of Iona, 'bards' were classed with 'beggars, vagabonds, and jugglers . . . to be put in the stocks and expelled from the district'. Today, the disincentives for Gaelic natural history are different. Perhaps the greatest is finding a readership able and willing to use and perpetuate the literature. Nonetheless, there is an opportunity awaiting the scholarly Gaelic naturalist to explore the literary and oral traditions of Gaelic natural history.

The Beatons had a hereditary medical tradition in Gaelic culture (Bannerman, 1986). They are thought to have come from Ireland about 1300 and became physicians to the Scottish kings, but were settled in the Isles. More of their medieval Gaelic manuscripts have survived than have any others, due mainly to the Rev John Beaton of Pennycross, Mull, who was the last learned member of the family. He listed the Beaton manuscripts, and was an informant of Edward Lhuyd the Keeper of the Ashmolean Museum, Oxford. Lhuyd (1660–1709) made a grand tour of the Celtic countries in 1697–1701, including Mull and Iona. He was backed by sponsors interested in archaeological, botanical, historical and linguistic material (Thompson, 1983). Lhuyd's collected manuscripts are now in the Library of Trinity College, Dublin. However, apart from John Beaton's knowledge and folklore taken down by Lhuyd (Campbell and Thompson, 1963) the etymologies of place names (Watson, 1926; Nicolaisen, 1976), and the names of the more conspicuous plants and animals (Hogan, 1900; Forbes, 1905; MacLeoid, 1976; Dwelly, 1977), little natural history exists in the Gaelic language.

18th and 19th Centuries

Classical natural history in Scotland has its origins in Edinburgh in the botanical and medical schools of Edinburgh University in the mid-17th century. The prime movers were Robert Sibbald and Andrew Balfour, both medical practioners, and they were followed by James Sutherland and John Hope, both, in their times, Professors of Botany at Edinburgh. Sibbald laid the foundation stone of Scottish natural history in his *Scotia Illustrata* (1684). However, it was not until the opening up of the Highlands by the roads and bridges built by General Wade after the Jacobite rising in 1715, that travellers gained easier and safer access to the Hebrides (Smout, 1969). Foremost among those who reached the Isles were Thomas Pennant (1769 and 1772) and Samuel Johnson with James Boswell (1773). In 1772, Pennant was accompanied by a botanist, the Rev John Lightfoot, who was librarian and chaplain to the Duchess of Portland, and there followed Lightfoot's *Flora Scotica* (1777–92) which included records from his travels in the Hebrides. This was the first serious botanical work on the Isles since the lists of plants by Lhyud (*c.* 1700), and it formed a botanical datum which is of relevance even today (Balfour 1979; Currie and Murray, 1983).

William MacGillivray was born in Aberdeen in 1796. Son of an army surgeon who was killed at Corunna in 1809, he spent much of his childhood at Northtown, the farm of his two paternal uncles in Harris. He attended the parish school at Obbe until he was eleven and then went to Aberdeen to enter the university at the age of twelve. His early experiences with wildlife in Harris fired his enthusiasm for natural science, which found expression in his fine *History of British Birds*, in three volumes, and his drawings of birds. His interests were mainly in ornithology, but he also followed the pearl fishers and noted the abundance of the pearl mussel (*Margaritifera margaritifera*) in the rivers of the Outer Hebrides (Waterston, 1981). From humble beginnings, MacGillivray rose to the Chair of Civil and Natural History in Aberdeen University. He had great physical endurance in the field, and had a reputation for outwalking his students on the hill. His paper, '*Account of a series of islands*

usually denominated the Outer Hebrides' (1830), was perhaps the
first professional zoological work on the Hebrides. In 1871,
Robert Gray laid a firm base for bird study in *The Birds of the
West of Scotland* to be followed in 1888 and 1892 by the *Vertebrate
Faunas* of J.A. Harvie-Brown and T.E. Buckley, and in 1890 by
The Birds of Iona and Mull by H.D. Graham.

Another signal event was the publication in 1873–74 of H.C.
Watson's *Topographical Botany* which set the framework of 112
Vice-Counties, of which the Inner Hebrides were numbered
(south to north) 102, 103 and 104, and the Outer Hebrides, 110.
This served to focus interest on the Isles as geographical units
in the study of the British flora, embodied the information
gained by many 19th century botanists, and attracted many
others to visit the Hebrides into this century. As far back as
1844, J.H. Balfour and C.C. Babington had recorded 349
species of flowering plant from the Outer Hebrides, and Watson's work was updated by A. Bennett in 1905. Andrew Currie
(1979) has described the advance in botanical recording in the
Hebrides from Watson's time through Ewing (1892–99), Trail
(1898–1909), Bennett (1905), Bennett *et al.* (1929–30), Druce
(1932) and Heslop-Harrison (1937–41) (Currie and Murray,
1983).

In the marine field, the earliest records come from a voyage
of the British Fishery Society to the Hebrides in 1787 but the
first species list for the littoral fauna was given by McIntosh in
1866, who also recognised the narrow frontiers between salt
and fresh waters in the Uists and the implications this might
have for the fauna. The *Lightning* and *Porcupine* expedition of
1869–70 and later, at the turn of the century, Marshall obtained
dredge samples from the sea-bed of the Hebridean shelf and
published the first accounts of the marine benthos (Jeffreys,
1879–84; Sykes, 1906–25; Marshall 1896–1912).

The 19th century was remarkable for the number of men and
women of private means who took their leisure in the rough
bounds of Scotland. Some of these were naturalists with a
passion for exploring the Hebrides, and foremost among them
was J.A. Harvie-Brown. He was a zealous writer of field notes,
journals and letters to many correspondents connected with
field-sports and natural history (p. 320). The *Vertebrate Faunas*
stand as milestones in Scottish natural history, and are
remarkably detailed and authentic, compiled from personal
notes or experiences, freshly remembered. These books,
though far outdated, have remained in use for a century; no
others have replaced them in the modern era. However, the
scholarship and altruism of Harvie-Brown was unusual, for the
cult of the sportsman-naturalist was basically romantic and
self-satisfying; it was about shared and solitary adventures in

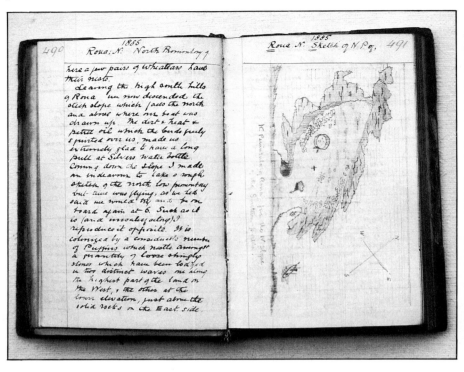

Pages of Harvie-Brown's journal showing a drawing of the Fianuis peninsula and notes of his visit to North Rona in 1887 (now in the Royal Museum of Scotland)

wild remote country, known (and owned) by a privileged few who were usually visitors for the season. Personal interpretations of the condition and behaviour of wild animals seen and hunted in the vastness of wilderness were fashionable, and often coloured by the knowledge and experience of gamekeepers and stalkers.

The life and works of Harvie-Brown and Robert Gray are to be the more honoured and valued when seen against those of the notorious collector of eggs and skins, Charles St John (1884 and 1893), described by Jean Balfour (1979) as 'the supreme example of the Victorian ornithologist with a gun', and of Osgood Mackenzie, whose book *A Hundred Years in the Highlands* is, *inter alia*, one of the best first-hand accounts ever written of the butchery of Highland wildlife. The toll taken of Hebridean wildlife by shooters, trappers, poisoners and collectors of all sorts over the last two centuries, is largely untold. However, there have been those among the landowners who were naturalists or early patrons of nature conservation, who encouraged these interests in their gamekeepers and sporting tenantry. Today, the Wildlife and Countryside Act is testimony to the historic mistrust which society, as a whole, has of those who live and work with wild creatures; the Act leaves little to the discretion of any person, irrespective of rank, about the length to which he or she may go, within the law, in disturbing, taking and killing wild species. However, law enforcement in the sparsely inhabited, be-misted Hebrides has never been easy. One of the Statutes of Iona (1609) stated—'No person to bear firearms outside his house or to shoot at deer, hares, or wildfowl, in accordance with Act of Parliament.' Yet only the clan chief himself was there to administer the law. Now, there are the SSPCA, RSPB, police, and a much more watchful and enlightened public, aware of the need to safeguard wildlife.

The Inner Hebrides have been most attractive to geologists for two centuries, and the enormous range of rock types and structures, spanning over two billion years, continues to provide an inexhaustible field of interest. MacCulloch (1819) remarks on the struggle he had to exclude repetitive detail from his descriptions of the Islands; yet his successors have served to put a level of detail in theses, papers and maps, such that there is hardly a corner of the Hebrides which has not been geologically explored and recorded. The 19th century spirit of geological exploration in the Hebrides was enshrined by Hugh Miller in *The Cruise of the Betsey* (1869), and the excitement and wonder of fossil-hunting in the Great Estuarine (Jurassic) rocks of Eigg (p. 36) and Skye (p. 322) in those far-off days, still makes enchanting reading. In this following passage he describes poignant moments of discovery at Ru Stoir on the north point of Eigg:

. . . I hammered lustily, and laid open in the dark red shale a vertebral joint, a rib, and a parellelogramical fragment of solid bone, none of which could have belonged to any fish. . . . The entire ribs I was lucky enough to disinter have, as in those of crocodileans, double heads; and a part of a fibula about four inches in length, seems also to belong to this ancient family. . . . I found the head of a flat humerus so characteristic of the extinct order to which the Plesiosaurus has been assigned . . . a range of skerries lay temptingly off, scarce a hundred yards from the water's edge: the shale beds might be among them, with Plesiosauri and crocodiles stretching entire; I fain would have swam off to them with my hammer in my teeth and my shirt and drawers in my hat, but the tall brown forest of kelp and tangle . . .

However, the most significant event in the scientific record of last century, was the publication in 1876 by the Ordinance Survey of the First Editions of the 'one-inch' (1:63,360) and 'six-inch' (1:10,560) maps. These provided the modern geographical base and a great stimulus to scientific survey and exploration when natural science most needed it, in the excitement of the Darwinian period. The Geological Survey was already in operation under Archibald Geikie, and the

The Elgol coast
geological SSSI, Skye.
R. N. Campbell
examines the polygonal
cracks in a fossil
mudflat of Jurassic
times about 160 million
years old (Photo
J. M. Boyd)

Bathymetrical Survey of the Freshwater Lochs by John Murray
and Laurence Pullar (1910) was shortly to follow.

The geological literature of the Hebrides is voluminous and
has increased greatly in the last 30 years. Lois Albert Necker,
born in Geneva in 1786, completed the earliest geological map
of Scotland, including the Hebrides, and his grave is in the old
churchyard at Portree. It is invidious to highlight the work of a
few in this welter of scientific endeavour by many. However,
there have been foci of great geological interest in Syke, the
Small Isles and Mull, not simply relating to the actual structures of the Islands, but also to the interpretation of the
elemental processes by which the rocks were formed. To
obtain a fair appreciation of all this great effort, reference
should be made to the *Geology of Scotland* (Ed. Craig, 1983).
Notable among the early works of this century were those of
J.E. Richey (1932) and co-workers in the 1920s, on the Tertiary
rocks of the Inner Hebrides, and Jehu and Craig (1923–34) on
the Lewisian of the Outer Hebrides. The vigourous follow-up
to that work after the war is reviewed respectively by Janet
Watson (1983) and C.H. Emeleus (1983), both of whom have
made substantial original contributions. Studies of the Torridonian, Moine, Dalradian, and Mesozoic rocks were focused
more on the mainland with extensions into the Hebrides.

First Half of the 20th Century

The 1930s saw the beginning of the modern period of scientific investigation, which received a great boost in the post-war revival of the 1950s. The effect of this revival is still felt, but in the last decade it has been diminished by a general reduction in the funding of research for purely scientific purposes. The Oxford–Cambridge Expedition to newly-evacuated St Kilda in 1931 was fired by the ecological movement that had evolved in the first three decades of this century (Sheail, 1987). The concept of the 'ecosystem' was uppermost in ecological thinking at that time, and attempts were being made to investigate how populations related to each other within circumscribed communities or habitats. To achieve this, whole communities required to be surveyed over periods of years, and where could these relationships be better demonstrated than on a small island? Possessing finite boundaries, severe limits to exchange of plants and animals (except migrant birds and insects), and having comparatively simple communities of plants and animals, the Hebrides were appealing—none more so than St Kilda, which at that time possessed the added dimension of 'release' from human habitation and livestock (Stewart, 1933). Some ecologists of the day saw in this an outstanding opportunity to observe, over the passage of years, the return of St Kilda to its pristine state—a prognosis which was partly frustrated by the re-introduction of sheep in 1932 (see p. 309), and the presence of a military garrison and organised parties of residential visitors since 1957. As it happens, we now understand that this was a fairly naive concept and that even though communities of plants and animals may well have inherent stable points towards which they will automatically track when released from the managerial influence of man, it is highly improbable that, once reached, the stable point will be anything like the one which existed before the arrival of man.

The appeal of islands to the ecologist as open-air laboratories influenced the thinking behind many other expeditions of scientific standing: Oxford and Cambridge Universities to St Kilda (1931) and Oxford to the Sound of Harris (Elton, 1938); Edinburgh University to Barra (1935) and St Kilda (1948); Durham University to many islands (1936–1956); Glasgow University to Canna (1936), Garvellachs (1951), St Kilda (1952 and 1956), and North Rona (1958). Over 30 years, ecological science had taken possession of a field previously worked by the naturalists, and this reflected the national trend. In modern times, this once profitable association of a professional science with an amateur pursuit still lingers, and unfortunately, does considerable harm when ecologists have to compete for funds with other professional scientists. Observation of the *systema naturae* on small islands, as pictured by Charles Elton (1949), is no longer in vogue. In 1957, when Rum (see p. 272) was purchased by the Nature Conservancy and St Kilda was acquired by the National Trust for Scotland, part of the reason for their existence as nature reserves was that they should be places where observations of the natural system could be carried out. Some observations still proceed, but they are small in scale from what was probably foreseen, and much of this kind of open-ended research is being forced to an end by shortage of funds. This provides a sharp contrast with the bounty of the times and optimism for the future of those bygone days, when funds and the fundamental relevance of what was being conceived were not in question.

The 1930s were a time of opportunism and disorder, into which came many enthusiasts, only a few of whom are remembered today. Fraser Darling, with an agricultural diploma, PhD, and Leverhulme and Carnegie Fellowships, studied the breeding behaviour of gulls on Eilein a'Chleirich in the Summer Isles, and grey seals on Lunga in the Treshnish Isles and North Rona (Boyd, 1986) (p. 324). Looked back at over half-a-century, his studies are those of an original pioneer, researching the middle ground between animal behaviour and ecology. He saw no pathway to truth in nature, other than being

Dr (later Sir) Frank Fraser Darling on Tanera Mor, Summer Isles in the early forties (Photo from Darling, 1944, Island Farm, Bell, London)

'at one' with wild creatures in the privacy of their own dwelling places and his main work was in the interface between man and nature. He was as much of a mystic as he was a scientist, who saw men and animals as parts of the same whole, and saw that man's moral and political make-up was an ecological factor capable of changing the entire character of nature. Later, he combined the knowledge gained in his agricultural and biological studies with his crofting experience on Tanera Mor, in the *West Highland Survey—An Essay in Human Ecology* (1955). However, the true and enduring effect of Fraser Darling's work is not to be found in the impact which his *West Highland Survey* had upon Government, but in the exciting challenge he gave to others, including us, through the most popular books of his Scottish period, *A Herd of Red Deer* (1937), *Island Years* (1940), *Crofting Agriculture* (1945), and *Natural History in the Highlands and Islands* (1947).

Another who is remembered from the 1920s and 1930s is Seton Gordon, the spirit of whose work was more romantic than scientific. He was in the mould of the 19th century naturalist of private means, who had a remarkable social cachet with gentry and crofter alike. *The Immortal Isles* (1926) and *Afoot in the Hebrides* (1950), two of his most important works on the Hebrides, are charming portraits of the Isles, their wildlife and people, but not works in natural history of the standing of Harvie-Brown or Fraser Darling. However, Seton Gordon made his home in Skye and, although not a Gaelic speaker, became a guru in island natural history, well known to a wider public through books and articles. He preceded the age of natural history as a popular feature on radio and television.

James Fisher made his name as an island-going naturalist in post-war radio and television, as well as from his books. He was an ornithologist and bibliographer with a great appetite for remote seabird islands, particularly St Kilda (p. 326). In the 1930s he started his surveys of gannets and fulmars (Fisher and Vevers, 1943–44; Fisher, 1952), which were to last a lifetime, and lead the great post-war surge in seabird research. Later, he became an editor of the New Naturalist Series. He had a contemporary in Robert Atkinson, whose adventures as a young naturalist on North Rona, St Kilda and Shillay (Harris) are told in *Island Going* (1949) and *Shillay and the Seals* (1980).

In the 1930s, natural history in the Hebrides became more attractive than ever before to a wider public, through naturalists like Seton Gordon and Fraser Darling, who were fine communicators of the aesthetic, as well as the scientific qualities of the Hebridean wildlife. Fraser Darling in his finest moments, however, saw in his work a deeper opportunity, akin to those who were not given to popular writing but to science

James Fisher on the island of Dun, St Kilda in 1948 (Photo H. Hope-Jones)

and scholarship. For example, Professor J.W. Heslop Harrison and the Durham University group over many years studied the taxonomic distinctiveness of the Hebrides, while others were amateur naturalists, like J.W. Campbell and his sister Miss M.S. Campbell who in their own quiet way had a great affinity for the Isles and, respectively, recorded birds and plants throughout their lives. Unfortunately, except for *The Flora of Uig* (1945) their works were never published, but their records have contributed greatly to subsequent studies (Cunningham, 1983; Currie, 1979). Miss Campbell's records are now in the British Museum (Natural History) and will be incorporated in a future *flora* of the Hebrides.

A.R. Waterston was a member of the Edinburgh party in Barra in 1933, and has continued to work on the non-marine invertebrates of the Outer Hebrides ever since. His *Non-marine invertebrate fauna of the Outer Hebrides* (1981) lays a basis

for all future invertebrate studies in the Hebrides, and provides a contribution to the natural history of Scotland. In this paper, he reviews the entire invertebrate literature for the Outer Hebrides from MacGillivray (1830) to Waterston and Lyster (1979). As regards the invertebrates of the Inner Hebrides, records exist from the mid-19th century onwards, but still await a compilation similar to that given by Welch (1983) to the coleoptera. Notable contributions were made by Balfour Brown (1953) between 1910 and 1953, and by J.W. Heslop-Harrison between 1939 and 1950, covering many taxa. Only Rum possesses a comprehensive inventory of invertebrates and has an exhaustive list of insects (Steel and Woodroffe, 1969; Wormell, 1982). J.L. Campbell (1970, *et seq.*, 1984) has recorded lepidoptera on Canna since the 1930s. There have also been naturalists in the marine field, notably A.C. Stephen and Edith Nicol (later Mrs. MacEwan of Muck) on the intertidal and brackish water fauna of the Uists, and J.E. Forrest and colleagues in Barra, in the 1930s. These were followed by J.R. Lewis in the 1950s and by many others after that (see Chapters 4 and 5).

The Fishery Research Vessel Explorer *from which much of the biological research in Hebridean waters was done from 1921 to 1956 (Crown Copyright)*

Second Half of the 20th Century

The 1950s saw a transition from the old style of descriptive natural history to the more modern scientific style of investigation, where it was more than the mere presence or absence of species that was important, it was the biological processes that allowed populations to grow and flourish or decline and go

extinct that were of interest. This has brought numerous
school and university expeditions to the Hebrides and led to
the establishment of several major programmes of research,
including those of the Nature Conservancy on the red deer on
Rum by V.P.W. Lowe and B. Mitchell, the grey seals of North
Rona by Morton Boyd and Niall Campbell and the Soay sheep
of St Kilda by Peter Jewell and Morton Boyd in collaboration
with workers from many different disciplines drawn from
research institutes throughout Britain. Work by Kenneth
Williamson and Morton Boyd on the vertebrate fauna of St
Kilda led to the publication of two books, *St Kilda Summer* and
A Mosaic of Islands, relating their experiences and discoveries
(p. 328).

The last forty years have brought funds and manpower on an
unprecedented scale to the study of the natural environment.
Before the Second World War, there were very few profes-

*J. M. B. with a storm
petrel photographed
against a tent on North
Rona in June 1958
(Photo J. MacGeoch)*

sional natural scientists in the Hebrides, but now there are many, advancing all sectors of environmental research with the aid of ships, boats, vehicles, aircraft and advanced technologies. We have taken part in this advance, in company with many of those named in the bibliographies of this book and its two main source volumes (Boyd, 1979; Boyd and Bowes, 1983). The following were some of the more important contributors, who were usually leaders of cognate groups.

In geology, there has been a particularly strong surge of research that reflects the wide range of geological time-scale, rock types and structures possessed by the Islands. R. Dearnley, D.J. Fettes, and Dr A.M. Hopgood have been prominent in the Lewisian, A.D. Stewart in the Torridonian, Dr J.D. Hudson in the Mesozoic, Dr A.C. Dunham, Dr C.H. Emeleus and R.N. Thompson in the Tertiary, J.B. Sissons in the Quaternary, and Dr G.E. Farrow in Recent Sediments. Professor W. Ritchie has illuminated the origin and development of dune-machair landforms.

In the botanical field, Andrew Currie and Mrs C.W. Murray, both resident in Skye, have carried out field studies of the flora, and tended the botanical record of the Hebrides over many years. Dr H.J.B. Birks and his wife, Dr H.H. Birks, have investigated the vegetational history through pollen analysis of sediments and peat, and have added to knowledge of the mosses. Dr R.E. Randall and Dr G. Dickenson have given descriptions of the flora and vegetation of the machair, and Professor D.H.N. Spence has done the same for the freshwater macrophytes. Botanical forays into the Isles by such experts as Dr R.W.G. Dennis and Dr R. Watling (fungi), Dr F. Rose and B.J. Coppins (lichens) and M.F.V. Corley (mosses) have greatly extended the inventory of the cryptogams. Notes on the flora of Tiree and Coll were made by U.V. Duncan, of Easdale and the Garvellachs by C.W. Muirhead, and of Mull by A.C. Jermy and J.A. Crabbe. Dr R.E.C. Ferreira produced a large-scale vegetation map of Rum, and Dr D.N. McVean and Dr D.A. Ratcliffe have described the community structure of the vegetation of the Hebrides, in the context of the Scottish Highlands and Islands.

In the zoological field, A.R. Waterston has continued his invertebrate studies, and a major survey was carried out on the invertebrates of dune and machair sites in Scotland in 1975–77, headed by Dr E.A.G. Duffey and Dr R.C. Welch. Peter Wormell has made a study of the lepidoptera of the Inner Hebrides, while R.N. Campbell and his son, Dr R.N.B. Campbell, have studied the distribution and ecology of freshwater fishes, including migratory salmon and trout. Their special interest has been the native species of Arctic charr and the 3- and 9-spined sticklebacks. R.M. Dobson has studied the natural history of Muck.

In the field of marine biology, Dr R. Mitchell, Dr R.C. Earll and Dr F.A. Dipper have developed the study of the seabed by diving methods, and studies of the littoral flora and fauna have been advanced by Professor T.A. Norton and H.T. Powell (algae), Dr S.M. Smith (molluscs) and I.S. Angus (beach fauna). Work on the marine mammals has been supported by R.W. Vaughan, Miss S.S. Anderson, C.F. Summers, N.W. Bonner and ourselves (seals), Dr P.G.H. Evans (whales) and James and Rosemary Green and Jane Twelves (otters).

W.A.J. Cunningham, Dr W.R.P. Bourne, Dr M.P. Harris, M.A. Ogilvie and T.M. Reed have carried out broadly based ornithological studies. Ornithology is by far the most popular

Richard Balharry strides up through the gannetry to the summit of the Stac Lee, St Kilda on 19th May 1969 — the first ascent of Stac Lee since the St Kildans left in 1930 (Photo J. M. Boyd)

pursuit in natural history, and the recent literature on the Hebrides bears the names of many, ourselves included, who have devoted much energy and time to the study of selected species, island populations, and migration. Notable among these was Kenneth Williamson, whose studies of the birds of St Kilda embraced the total breeding population of the islands, the autoecology of the St Kilda wren and the snipe (*Gallinago gallinago faeroeensis*), and the first account of migration through Hirta. Notable also are the works of R.L. Swan and D.A.K. Ramsay on the birds of Canna, and C.G. Booth on Islay. There were many key works on selected species of bird with the main focus in the Hebrides: Dr J. Cadbury on corncrakes; R.J. Fuller on waders; Dr. P. Monaghan and Dr E. Bignall on choughs; S. Murray, Dr S. Wanless and Dr J.M. Boyd on gannets; J.A. Love and R.H. Dennis on sea-eagles; Dr D.A. Stroud on Greenland white-fronted geese, P. Wormell on Manx shearwaters, and others.

The taxonomic distinctiveness of species living in island isolation has excited the curiosity of biologists since the publication of the *Origin of Species*. The Hebrides have their own genetical idiosyncrasies, which were brought to notice by James Ritchie in his celebrated book *The Influence of Man on Animal Life in Scotland* (1920), and we have already mentioned the work of Professor Heslop Harrison in this field. More recently, these island populations in the Hebrides have been examined by Professor R.J. Berry, in the context of wider genetical studies of the fauna of the Scottish islands, and by Professor M.J. Delany in his ecological studies of field-mice. The detailed studies of the reproductive physiology, ecology and behaviour of red deer on Rum firstly by Professor R.V. Short and Dr G.A. Lincoln, and later by Dr T.H. Clutton-Brock, Miss F.E. Guinness and Dr S.D. Albon, and similarly on Soay sheep at St Kilda by Professor P.A. Jewell, have international standing in science.

The total sum of knowledge gained from all this research is enormous. Today, the scientific record of the Hebrides would be far beyond the dreams of MacCulloch, MacGillivray, Geikie and Harvie-Brown, but it is a fulfilment of the aspirations of Fraser Darling, James Campbell, Balfour-Browne and James Ritchie, all of whom saw the dawn of the new age.

CHAPTER 4

Land Use—Tryst of Man
and Nature

Land Use History

The earliest people in the Hebrides lived by the shore. There
was an abundance of food, fuel, and shelter, and when
resources became locally exhausted, they moved on, leaving
the deserted dwelling-place to recover its natural complexion.
As time advanced however, and the numbers of people
increased, the land became fully possessed and settled. Laws of
tenure and use evolved, all of which affected the distribution of
wealth, and the social structure. Population pressures and political factors resulted in the extension of agricultural settlement
from fertile coastal land into the interior of the islands, with
cultivation of moorland, and this extension continued until the
gradual introduction of the crofting system between 1800 and
1830. At the time of its inception, crofting aimed to improve
agricultural standards and to sustain the high population
employed in the kelping (Caird, 1979)—an industry that
collapsed after the end of the Napoleonic Wars. In Islay and
Gigha, the extension of agriculture into the interior resulted in
a permanent change in the interior of the islands, but elsewhere much of the land and settlement became derelict. In the
late 18th and 19th centuries, the creation of large farms
displaced crofters and cottars from the most fertile land, caus-
ing great congestion and overworking of the land in the surviv-
ing crofting townships (Fig. 1).

In Islay, these changes began in the middle of the 18th
century, lasted a century, and produced a non-crofting
environment of lowland character (Storrie, 1981). Elsewhere in the Hebrides, this period saw the conversion of
the chaotic 'run-rig' system (p. 113, H-ANT) into either
crofting or farming units, often organised side by side as
on Canna (see below). The existing medieval system of
small farms with many tenants, who worked unenclosed
strips of arable and grazing common land, was gradually
reorganised into crofts, which possessed a small acreage of
enclosed arable, and a share in a large acreage of common
grazing; or else the land was cleared of such tenants to
form a single large farm. The whole industry of crofting

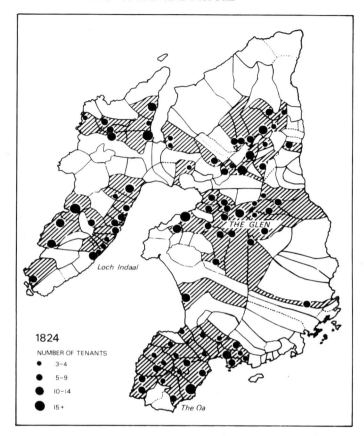

1824

NUMBER OF TENANTS

● 3-4

● 5-9

● 10-14

● 15+

Fig. 1
In 1824, an Islay Estate rental shows that the island still had over 60 multiple townships, shared and worked by over 700 tenants (Islay Estate Papers quoted by Storrie, 1983)

was thoroughly researched by Dr James Hunter in *The Making of the Crofting Community* (1976). However, each island has its own melancholy chronicle of this time, which can be pieced together from estate papers, the Statistical Account of Scotland (1845) and the National Censuses. Another scholarly work, *Canna* by Dr John Lorne Campbell (1984), tells the story of one island upon which we now draw for illustration.

The events which brought about the clearance of Canna in 1851, when probably about half of the 238-strong population left for Canada, began with the sale of all his estates by Reginald George MacDonald of Clanranald in the early 19th century. This affected great areas of Moidart, Small Isles, the Uists and Benbecula. Canna and Sanday were purchased in 1827 by the then tenant, Donald MacNeill, for £9,000. MacNeill's first action as owner was to emigrate some 200 inhabitants at his own expense, and reorganise the agricultural holdings in the home farm and many crofts; squatting and subdivision of holdings were prohibited. However progressive this may appear, there was continuous poverty and destitution, which was greatly aggravated by the potato blight in 1845–50, and by the leasing of the island to a flockmaster from Moidart who, finding the executors of estate financially weak, insisted on the eviction of crofters from Canna as a condition of lease. Accordingly in 1851, the tenants of Keills were evicted and those at Tarbert and Sanday retained.

The potato famine is graphically described by Hunter (1976) and Devine (1988). Following a bumper crop in 1845, during which some 15,410 barrels of potatoes were exported from Tobermory, the weather of the spring and early summer of 1846 greatly favoured the spores of the fungus *Phytophthora infestans*. In critical warm, moist conditions, a single plant infected by the fungus can infect thousands in a few hours of light winds; the multiplier-effect is very rapid.

The famine struck first in Harris where the previous year's potatoes had rotted in the storage pits, leaving the people seriously short of food in advance of the new crop, which, in turn, was completely blighted. The famine was widespread. People were bewildered and, already impoverished, completely unprepared for such an emergency. Starvation and outbreaks of typhus, cholera, and dysentery were to follow in a crisis which took many years to overcome.

The primary aim of the landowners in many islands was the maintenance of the high revenues of the kelp industry; the effi-

Fig. 2
Land use in South Boisdale, South Uist 1805–1977 (from Caird 1979)

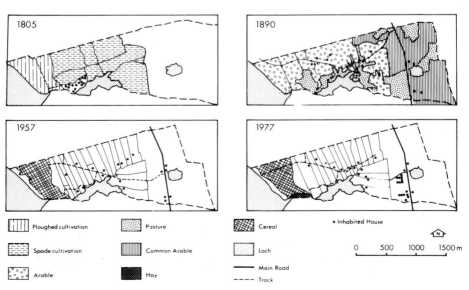

ciency of agriculture was not raised for its own sake, nor from
any altruistic motive. Many areas of wet machair were drained
and areas of spade cultivation on moorland were abandoned to
sheiling pasturage. The patterns of small-holdings (Fig. 2) of
all shapes and sizes mixed with the larger farms gave a high
level of diversity to the cultivated landscape, while the regimes
of grazing and burning of hill land tended to reduce the
diversity of moorland habitats. This variety within the culti-

Fig. 3
*Cropping and livestock
changes in the Outer
Hebrides 1870–1970
(from Caird, 1979)*

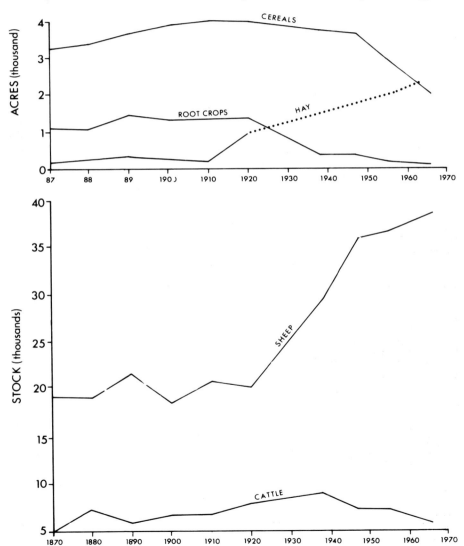

vated lands was enhanced by patchworks of rotational cropping, with grass leys of widely differing ages, and further enhanced by the wide range of individual crofting styles, from the neglected to the well-worked holding. The ecology of the Islands was therefore substantially changed by the crofting system, and their character as a habitat for wildlife was determined for at least a century to come.

Over the last century the pattern of land tenure has changed in Tiree, Raasay, much of Skye and the Outer Hebrides, where almost all of the large farms created during the Clearances were restored to crofting tenure between 1900 and 1930. In other parts of the Hebrides, land was acquired by the state for resettlement, and today there are over 1,000 crofting tenants on state-owned land. There was a similar resettlement on private land with state assistance, and the overall effect was to create several thousand new holdings and a much higher level of diversity of agricultural habitats. Agricultural output has also changed considerably (Fig. 3). The cropping regimes of arable crops and livestock remained remarkably steady until the end of the First World War, after which there were great increases in the numbers of sheep relative to cattle, and much more hay relative to root crops. After the Second World War, numbers of sheep remained high, while cattle numbers declined, and at the same time cereals have been greatly reduced in favour of grass production for hay and silage. Nonetheless, the agricultural regimes have been unrelenting in the toll that they have taken from the land since medieval times. Scythed cereals and hay, with potatoes and turnips cultivated by plough and spade and manured with seaweed, was the mixed regime of last century. Today, it is replaced by mechanised grass-intensive systems providing permanent pasture, baled hay, silage, and small plots of cereals (barley, oats, and rye) and potatoes, raised mainly on artificial fertilisers. The climate and soil conditions tend to maintain the drift of sand, choke the drains with luxuriant vegetation and degrade fences. Any decline in the vigour of the island communities in the upkeep of their land soon shows in blow-outs of sand, beds of rushes, gimcrack fences and wandering livestock.

Agricultural Improvement

In the 1960s, surface seeding was carried out on some 6,100ha. of hill pasture in the Outer Hebrides. The technique was especially well-suited for conditions in Lewis, but some hill land was also treated in the Uists. Shell-sand was transported from the shore and spread on the moorland, followed by

compound fertiliser and a clover/grass seed mixture. The resulting green pastures were thereafter grazed mostly by cattle, and booster treatments of shell-sand were given. Most of these pastures are now over twenty years old. A survey of 101 of them in Lewis in 1975 gave the following percentage frequencies (Grant, 1979):

The reclamation of peatland in Lewis by fencing and treatment with shell-sand, compound fertiliser, and a seed mixture of grasses and clovers, for improved cattle pasture (Photo J. M. Boyd)

Rye grass	Tim- othy	Meadw grass	White clover	Yorks fog	Other grass	Other specs	Bare gd & moss
2.6	0.2	9.0	20.1	10.3	14.7	27.6	15.5

Though many of these pastures have become rush infested, others have not, and all of them have an ecology that is distinct from the moorland context. They are now part of the 'blackland' zone between machair and hill and containing ingredients of both. For example, they are attractive to greylag geese, lapwing, snipe, redshank, skylark, meadow pipit and wheatear.

Crofting has never attracted sufficient investment to provide the development of machinery, seeds and livestock especially suited to its small-scale purposes in islands exposed to high, salt-laden winds. For example, modern ploughs are unsuitable for seedbed preparation on the light soils; the smallest combine harvester, unlike the old-fashioned binder, is too large a machine for small-field harvesting. Another example is the finding of a suitable cereal for machine cropping. In trials in the Uists, the Welsh black oat proved to give more straw and twice the grain yield of the local 'small oats' (*Avena strigosa*). However, due to lack of a market, the Welsh suppliers gave up, and the grain was lost to the Hebrides.

Blackface are the preferred breed of sheep for the open hill ranges and the Cheviot or Cheviot X Blackface for the machairs and improved pastures. The fertile islands of Lismore and Tiree will each produce about 5,000 lambs annually, the former mainly Blackface X Cheviot/Leicester, the latter mainly Cheviot X Leicester/Suffolk, and there is an even wider range of cross-bred cattle. The traditional Highland breed, of which there are pure bred herds on Rum and Canna, has been crossed with the Shorthorn to produce a hardy cow (Luing breed) which may be crossed with other beef breeds. The dairy industry in Islay, however, is supported mainly by Ayrshire and Friesian herds. All the livestock has been selected from mainland breeds, and none, with the possible exception of the Highland and Luing cattle, have been bred for conditions on the western seaboard of Scotland.

In 1982, a five-year Integrated Development Programme (IDP) was approved for the 'Western Isles', the island-authority area of Comhairle nan Eilein, which in this book is the 'Outer Hebrides'. In the programme as initially cast, no financial provision was made for the care of the environment, though such was sought from the EEC. Later, funds were made available for the NCC to carry out an appraisal of the environmental consequences of the IDP, and in particular its effect on wildlife. Field surveys were quickly organised, and a report drawing on the results of these was produced for the NCC by Dr J. Hambrey (1986). Conservation bodies argued successfully that more resources be made available, in the provisions of the Wildlife and Countryside Act, 1981, to appoint field staff and pay compensation to crofters on SSSIs, when foregoing IDP financial benefits for the sake of wildlife.

The IDP, therefore, gave an opportunity to revitalise agriculture in the Outer Hebrides, which had never known the prosperity of farming on the mainland, and which had become seriously undermanned. It was expected, therefore, that the effect of the Programme might be muted by the limited capacity of the community to respond to schemes to improve soil conditions for livestock husbandry. The main operations were draining, fertilising and reseeding of permanent grassland and moorland, use of herbicides and the repair of fences. Fencing proved most popular, with expenditure of over £5 million in grants.

The IDP was *prima facie* a beneficent measure which, if it had been carried too far, might have caused damage to wildlife. Contractors using heavy machinery could drain large areas with a speed and efficiency never dreamt of by the men of the last century with their draining spades. Also, the widespread mechanical application of artificial fertilisers, herbicides and mixtures of seeds on the flowery, bird-rich machairs and old hay meadows, some freshly drained, could substantially change the habitat of the islands.

Dr Hambrey's analysis is an object lesson about the effects of agricultural development on the natural environment. Important in this is the degree to which development could proceed so as to cause no damage to wildlife (and in certain respects be beneficial), and the setting of thresholds of effect beyond which development is damaging. However, the determination of both requires much research. (Much of this was put in hand, and is described in Chapters 6 and 7 of H-ANT.

Public opinion was polarised. At one pole there were those in the conservation bodies, who had seen the demise of wildlife by the agricultural transformation of the countryside in mainland Britain, and who feared that the same might happen in the Outer Hebrides—species like the corncrake, which has virtually disappeared from mainland Britain and still survives in the Hebrides, became a symbol of the conservation cause in the IDP. At the other pole, were the local people and their agricultural and political advisers, whose concerns were in livelihood and increased prosperity in what, in EEC terms, was one of the 'less-favoured areas' of Europe.

The Hambrey report *Agriculture and Environment in the Outer Hebrides* states:

Fortunately, this potential for damage to the environment has not, so far, been realised, with drainage and reseeding activity still on the 'beneficial or neutral' side of the damage threshold.

It seems clear now that the worst fears of the conservation bodies have not been confirmed by events in the five years of the IDP. The IDP did not extend to the Inner Hebrides, which at that time benefited only from the normal regime of agricultural subsidy. Yet, even without such a campaign as the IDP, the wetlands of Tiree have been drained in the last ten years with changes in the vegetation and breeding birds as great, or greater than, can be found under the IDP.

The IDP in the Outer Hebrides has now been followed by an Agricultural Development Programme (ADP) for the Inner Hebrides (and Orkney and Shetland). The lessons learnt in environmental care in the IDP have been ploughed into arrangements for the ADP, which is for the period 1988–93. One of the objectives of the ADP is to promote and provide opportunities for agriculturists to maintain the high environmental quality of the islands. Perhaps the most important advance from the IDP is the provision in the ADP of funds for

Hay ricks in a croft in Sleat, Skye (Photo J. M. Boyd)

'environmental management payments,' by which valued wildlife and landscape features can be conserved with rational agricultural development. The following are eligible habitats: over-grazed and over-burned heather, herb-rich grassland on limestone or base-rich soils; woodland and scrub, both existing and newly planted; margins of open water; wet areas waterlogged for 9 months or more per year; wildlife corridors such as burnsides, ditches, and field margins; steep rocky ground within inbye land; and winter keep in a mosaic of cereal, root, and grass crops. This imaginative approach offers great opportunities over five years for experimental management of crofts and farms in the islands, mainly for livestock and wildlife and to establish a new enlightened format for island landuse into the next century.

On Islay the improvement of grassland and dairy livestock husbandry in the past thirty years has been accompanied by an increase in the numbers of barnacle geese spending the winter on that island. We have given an outline of the natural history of this increase (Chapter 4, H-AMI); here we consider the landuse implications of the dual management of land for farm stock and wild geese.

In 1981, the Wildlife and Countryside Act placed a duty upon the NCC to offer management agreements to owners and occupiers of SSSIs, whose operations might cause damage to wildlife. Accordingly, the main goose-feeding areas of Gruinart Flats, Bridgend Flats and Laggan Peninsula having been

notified as SSSIs in 1983, the NCC was able to offer a measure
of compensation to the farmers within these SSSIs. The aim
was to stop shooting and allow the geese freedom to graze the
improved grasslands. Agreement was difficult, since there was
no existing code of values which gave a standard of equivalence
between domesticated stock and wild geese, and at first it did
not seem possible to reach agreement, but continuing negotia-
tions resulted in some farmers and landlords receiving compensation from September 1985, providing that geese were not
shot on any of their land that lay within the SSSIs.

The ultimate success of the scheme rests largely on the hope
that, in due time, the conditions prevailing in the SSSIs, where
there is ample nutritious food and no shooting, will prove suffi-
ciently attractive to draw the geese away from farms lying outside the SSSIs. Under present legislation, farmers whose land
lies outside SSSIs cannot receive compensation, but can obtain
a licence to shoot barnacle geese in protection of their crops.
The SSSIs cover the areas of greatest impact, but not all land
visited by geese in the course of the winter. Where the boundary of the SSSI includes one farm and excludes its neighbour,
there can be a sense of grievance felt by the farmer outside,
who cannot be offered a management agreement by the NCC,
who receives no compensation, who has to seek a licence to
shoot the barnacles, and has the task of flighting the flocks from
his land.

The difficulties in obtaining a satisfactory scheme which will
be fair to all are great. However, this is breaking new ground in
nature conservation and farming, and it is vital that all who are
responsible for devising and implementing the scheme should
see themselves in the forefront of experimental landuse, where
stocks of wildlife and farm animals can be successfully managed for the benefit of both, nowhere more so than at Gruinart
where the RSPB Reserve is set cheek-by-jowl with a dairy
farm. The RSPB has a wildfowl reserve managed as a livestock
farm; the local farmer has a livestock farm managed as a goose
reserve.

Forestry

In the Sub-boreal period about 3,500 years ago, the climate was
warmer, drier and probably less windy than it is today, and the
natural forest in the islands was at its peak of development. It
was dominated throughout by birch, but there were oak-
dominated woods in the Inner Hebrides. The variety of native
species that we see today in the remnants of old woodland
(Chapter 8, H-ANT), were probably all present in much

greater measure in the old forest. Ash, wych elm, alder, willow, hazel, rowan, gean, aspen and holly were all present within the birch and oak woods. About 2,500 years ago, the Sub-Atlantic period brought a colder, wetter and windier climate than before, and this was accompanied by a substantial regression of forest cover. The adverse climate, coupled with the exploitation of the forest by Neolithic cultivators and pastoralists, and later by Viking invaders and settlers, made the Hebrides almost treeless by the end of the Norse period in 1263.

The woodlands that regenerated on the sheltered sides of the larger Inner Hebrides in medieval times were cut in the 17th and 18th centuries to provide charcoal for iron smelting, mainly at Bonawe in Lorne, and much of this resulted in coppice management of oakwoods. The First Statistical Account (1792–96) records limited areas of natural woodland in Mull and Skye, and first mention is made of plantations in Skye and Raasay. By the time of the New Statistical Account (1845), plantations of mixed conifers and broadleaves were recorded in Islay, Jura, Mull, Skye and Raasay. The common conifers in these early plantations were Norway spruce (*Picea abies*), European larch (*Larix decidua*), Scots pine (*Pinus sylvestris*) and less commonly, Douglas fir (*Pseudotsuga menziesii*). Among the broadleaves, sycamore (*Acer pseudoplatanus*) was by far the most popular plantation tree, but oak, ash, beech (*Fagus sylvatica*) and Norway maple (*Acer platanoides*) were also planted (see p. 148). These plantations were carefully established and tended, but

A maturing forestry plantation mainly of Sitka spruce in Glen Varragill, Skye. Today, such a plantation would have within it a measure of broadleaved trees which would improve its appearance and wildlife (Photo C. Maclean)

by the 1880s they had fallen into neglect because of agricultural depression and cheap imported timber. There was also much coppicing of natural woods, which later became pasture woodlands for sheep and deer. Aged survivors stand today at Ardura (Mull), Ord and Leitir-Fura (Skye), and other old woods, which we have named in Chapter 8 of H-ANT. Today it is very difficult to establish broadleaved trees on open hillsides in the Hebrides, as the sylvicultural work on Rum has shown. However, it is possible within a 'nursery' plantation of conifers.

Until the late 1930s, the *raison d'etre* for planting was the build-up of the strategic reserve. By 1938, however, thought was being given to forestry as a means of giving social and employment benefits to depopulated areas. In the mid-1950s, forestry was conceived as an adjunct to crofting, and Fraser Darling had given encouragement to this in *West Highland Survey* (1955). The Forestry Commission responded in Mull, Skye and Jura by planting land that would only grow a lower than average crop, to provide ancillary employment to crofters. These acquisitions had small areas of land suitable for planting, interspersed among large areas, which were deemed unsuitable, but which would be kept in agricultural use. However, the scheme perished on the rocks of technological advance in sylviculture and the intricacies of crofting land tenure. The Commission had produced strains of lodgepole pine (*Pinus contorta*) and Sitka spruce (*Picea sitchensis*) which made planting possible on sites deemed 'unplantable'. This resulted in the planting of larger blocks of conifers and more completely afforested landscapes than intended.

A. G. Bramwell and G. M. Cowie (1983) gave details of planting until 1981 in the Inner Hebrides, which we summarise in Table 1. In the Outer Hebrides at the same date, there were 624ha. planted and 175ha. in hand for planting, all in Lewis (R. C. B. Johnstone, pers.comm).

Island	Plantation	Land to be Planted	Total
Skye*	8,712	3,448	12,160
Mull	9,930	2,602	12,532
Jura	672	304	976
Islay	845	1,356	2,201
Total	20,159	7,710	27,869

*including Raasay

Table 1   The areas (ha.) in the Inner Hebrides of both Forestry Commission and private land, which were under plantation and scheduled for planting, in March 1981. (Compiled from Bramwell and Cowie, 1983).

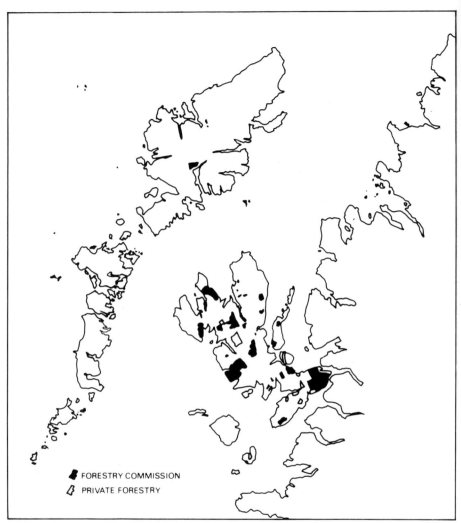

Fig. 4 *a & b*
Maps showing the
distribution of Forestry
Commission and
private forestry in the
Hebrides (from
Forestry Commission
maps)

In 1981, approximately three-quarters of the 27,800 ha.
acquired at that time for production forestry had been
planted; there were 20,160 ha. in plantations and 7,710 ha. in
hand for planting. Plantations in Mull were the most
advanced, and when all the land in hand for planting has been
stocked with trees, some 14% of the island will be afforested,
compared with 7% in Skye, 3% in Islay and 2% in Jura.
Bramwell and Cowie give some indication of further potential
(ha. plantable) for commercial forestry in the Inner Hebrides
as follows:

Island	Skye*	Mull	Jura	Islay	Total
Hectares	21,000	15,000	12,000	12,000	60,000

*including Raasay

If this potentially afforestable land is added to the 1981 totals it would account for 20% of the land surface of Mull, 18% of Skye, 31% of Jura and 23% of Islay. However, there are constraints against such large areas being afforested. Since 1981, a strong adverse public reaction has occurred in Scotland to new large-scale afforestation schemes, particularly in areas of high scenic and wildlife value. Research into public attitudes by the Scottish Forestry Trust points to this reaction being from 'interest groups' rather than from the general public. Nevertheless, it is real, and in our experience, massive. Such adverse reaction might be found in Mull where the plantations are large and are part of a much larger afforested landscape including Fuinary and Morven. In the Hebrides as a whole, however, tree cover is scarce and planting is favoured. The islands have their own indigenous obstacles to extensive afforestation on remote, exposed sites on crofting land, and a significant proportion of the plantable land is the common grazing of crofters which is retained for animal husbandry. Unless the current recession in agriculture results in a relaxation of the restraints on afforestation of crofting land, large areas will remain unplanted. The same restraint does not apply to farmland and deer forest. One of the greatest disincentives to crofter forestry arises from the fact that, despite favourable terms of purchase of crofts by the tenant crofter, few have chosen to own their croft, and as a consequence, any trees which are planted on a tenanted croft belong to the landowner and not the crofter.

The ability of the forest industry to plant Sitka spruce and lodgepole pine extensively in the Inner Hebrides and in the northern Outer Hebrides should not be underestimated. A recent symposium (Henderson and Faulkner, 1987) showed the enormous scientific and technical endeavour that supports the advance of Sitka spruce as the ideal timber species for north-western Britain. It is a native of the west coast fog-belt of North America which thrives in the oceanic climate of Britain. With a high level of tolerance to wind exposure, it resists windthrow better than others and adjusts successfully to a wide range of soil conditions. It is not beyond the sylviculturalist to produce a strain of Sitka spruce that will withstand the rigours of the Hebrides and produce a crop of timber, albeit at high cost and driven by a strong political will to do so in adverse conditions — for example, in an effort to create jobs. Today, the Forestry Commission is more active in the Outer Hebrides than ever before on objectives other than the production of an economic crop of timber.

Much depends on how new plantings and restockings are done to maintain the varied character of the Islands; by the use of small well-landscaped plantations; the sparing of important wetland areas; the provision of wide irregular margins of roads, streams, lochs and deer glades; the encouragement of habitat diversity by the use of broadleaved species, and the positive conservation of species and habitat by the establishment of woodland reserves and schemes for the encouragement of rare plant and insect life, nesting birds and bats.

However, these measures, which are now commonplace in commercial forestry in the uplands and islands, come too late to have any effect on plantations established before 1970. The first fifty years of commercial forestry based on the build-up of a strategic reserve of home-grown timber and, in the Scottish Highlands and Islands, with regard to social and economic benefits, paid little attention to needs of nature conservation as we know them today. The argument that forests of exotic conifers confer as many benefits as disadvantages to wildlife depends on what value is placed on the natural features removed or obscured by afforestation, as compared with others which forestry creates. The conservation movement lays a far greater value on rare and endangered native species and habitats, than it does on alien species and habitats, even though these may abound with native plants and animals. The whole concept, however, requires to be placed in relation to the growth cycle of the forest. In the early seedling and thicket stages, the plantations have greatly increased stocks of wildlife, which dwindle as the trees grow and the canopy closes, and in the dense pole and thinning stages, the wildlife content is greatly reduced.

Early planters of trees in the Hebrides tended to avoid deep peat and espoused free-draining brown earths and peaty gleys, with a good deal of mineral till. Now that deep peat is deemed economically plantable with Sitka spruce and lodgepole pine, the few hitherto undisputed mires have come within reach of afforestation, and whatever benefit may be conferred by such plantations, the mires from which they have grown will have been changed for ever. The rarity of such mires in the Hebridean biome makes such a loss too high a price to pay, in conservation terms, for the trees that the land will bear. The most valuable of these sites have now become SSSIs (Chapter 6), but it is important in the conservation of the wildlife and scenic character of the Hebrides, that the land outside SSSIs be afforested with a view to conserving the natural features within the mix of landuses: for example, by sparing bold fluvio-glacial features which are familiar and well-liked local landmarks; bogs with pool and hummock systems, which possess habitats now seldom found elsewhere; the breeding flats of greenshank, of which there are only about 70 pairs in the Hebrides; the nesting lochs of divers which have low breeding success and require flyways well clear of trees; and the banks of streams which are linear species-rich habitats of high diversity. Though there is no evidence as yet from northern Scotland, the acidification of soils and freshwaters by acid rain may be exacerbated by coniferous plantations, and the effects may be buffered by the ditches out-flowing upon the land surface at least 20m from the stream. All of these measures are embodied in several advisory publications by the Forestry Commission (1986, 1988), and the Royal Society for the Protection of Birds (1985) on the management of conifer and broadleaved woodlands.

Also, the increase of exotic tree species should not be at the expense of the existing natural broadleaved woodlands of birch, oak, ash, hazel, willow and other native species. As many of these woods as possible should be included within forestry fences, left unplanted and naturally regenerated. Those which have been underplanted might have the conifers removed, as is being done by the Forestry Commission in the fine broadleaved wood at Leitir-Fura east of Loch na Dal, Skye. The plantations could also contain a proportion of native broadleaved species (apart from volunteers along the woodland edges), similar to the experimental plots on Rum (Chapter 15).

Today, agriculture is declining and forestry advancing in Britain. The Budget of 1988 announced the end of the tax-incentive system of support to forestry. In its place has come a new Woodland Grants Scheme, with increased grants to compensate the industry for the loss of the tax benefits. More authority is given to the Forestry Commission by the admin-istration of the increased grant, accompanied by a system of environmental assessment with conservation and other guidelines, and incentives are given to farmers and crofters to plant more trees. This will be particularly attractive in Islay, Jura, Mull and Skye, but may also affect Lewis and Harris. If this increase is handled with the necessary stops and balances mentioned above, serious loss of wildlife and scenic values will be prevented, while the industrial base of the islands might be extended and employment of local people enhanced. Many of the Inner Hebrides are locally infested with bracken (*Pteridium aquilinum*) which causes serious illness in cattle, pigs and horses, but less so in sheep and deer. Continuous grazing and burning of the hill ground over centuries has encouraged the spread of bracken on well-drained slopes suitable for growing trees, but one rotation of conifers (*c.* 50 years) on such ground will eliminate bracken *in extenso* and provide a fresh start for agriculture, if that is preferred to restocking the clean land with trees (Fletcher and Kirkwood, 1982).

In 1969–79, the Red Deer Commission recorded a 26% increase in the red deer population of Mull, not including those in woodland. In the same period, 4,000ha. of open deer range were enclosed for forestry. The disruption of, and hardship to, the deer herds caused by enclosing land for forestry in the Highlands, can be reduced by enlightened choice of land for planting and by culling the deer, particularly hinds. Stags are the sporting attraction and are generally well culled, but hind culling is not attractive to the sportsman and is often neglected, and this long-sustained neglect is now at the centre of the serious over-population of the Highlands and Islands by red deer.

When deer enter plantations they prosper, cause damage to the trees and are very difficult to control. Sadly, the knowledge, skill, manpower and funds for efficient deer control are often lacking and difficult to apply in Highland estates. To achieve success in forestry, deer must be excluded from young plantations. Deer-proof fences seldom last more than 20 years, and the maturing forests become refuges and feeding ranges of red and roe deer. The interaction of forestry and red deer is an ever-present factor in Highland land use, and it makes timber enterprises less economically-worthwhile and ecologically difficult to manage. A great deal of research has been done since the last war to describe the behaviour of red deer in commercial plantations, and to assess the damage they do to various crop species at different stages of forest growth (Jenkins, 1986).

Minerals

The varied geology of the Hebrides is reflected in the large variety of economic minerals which are found in the islands. There are ores of iron, lead, and chromite; silica-rich rocks; diatomite; aggregates of limestone, fine-grained sandstone, sands and gravels. Though large quantities of these minerals are generally present, with the exception of sands and gravels, they are usually in beds too thin to be economically workable, or are too 'impure' for industrial use (Gribble, 1983). There are quartz crystal, agate and jasper; garnetiferous and sapphire-bearing rocks; bloodstone in Rum and greenstone (serpentine marble) in Tiree and Iona.

Ores

The Raasay ironstone bed is about 2m thick, and it outcrops in the south-east of the island for about 12km, from the Inverarish Burn in the south, along the cliff face to Screapadal in the north, with another 2km outcrop off-set in Beinn na'Leac. Total reserves are thought to be between 10 and 16 million tonnes of ironstone, of which only about 0.3 million tonnes have so far been worked. It is a low grade ore which was mined between 1914 and 1919, and the remains of the workings can be seen today near Raasay Pier. There are also concentrations of magnetite on Tiree and Skye. On Tiree, the 4m-thick band has been traced for 7km from Loch a'Phuill to Loch Bhasapol and contains reserves of over 3 million tonnes of ore. The magnetite goes to a depth of 80m, is masked by drift deposits and is thought to disperse into narrow strands and to be commercially unworkable. On Skye, there are some 20 small pockets of magnetite in the contact zone between the granite of Beinn an Dubhaich and the Durness limestone in Strath.

Veins of lead occur in limestones of the Dalradian rocks of Islay which have been worked since the 16th century. These massive gangues of limestone containing concentrations of

The Torrin marble quarry showing a basalt sill in the Cambrian marble above granophyre (Photo British Geological Survey)

galena (native lead sulphide) occur in the north-east of the island and were mined north of Loch Finlaggan between 1860 and 1880, when only about 2,260 tonnes of ore were removed (Gribble, 1983). Chromite occurs in the Tertiary intrusive rocks of Skye and Rum, where dispersed grains occur within the olivine-rich facies, occasionally aggregating into layers of up to 25mm thick which are not commercially workable.

Silica

The quartzites of Jura, Islay and Skye may contain some sizeable concentrations of very pure silica. The purest deposit in Scotland is the 6m-thick bed of white cretaceous sandstone at Loch Aline, which produces some 75,000 tonnes of crushed stone annually. This bed has stratigraphical relations with similar, but thinner, beds of sandstone in western Mull. Analysis shows that the Loch Aline sandstone is 99.69% silica, compared with 98.04% for the Cambrian basal quartzite at Ord, Skye, and 97.89% for shore sand in Jura, and 95.73% for Dalradian quartzite on the shore at Bunnahabhainn, Islay. The 'Singing Sands' of Camus Sgiotaig in Eigg, derived from the local Jurassic sandstone, also have a very high silica content.

Diatoms are microscopic, unicellular phytoplankton that are encased in silica. Their remains accumulate as marine and lacustrine deposits and, in geological time, form beds of white diatomite, which is used in filters, fire-resistant materials and as a light-weight filler. Nine sites of diatomite occur in Trotternish, Skye. These deposits are small, partially worked-out and, except for that at Loch Mealt (which would require to be drained) uneconomic. Small deposits of diatomite also occur in North Tolsta and North Shawbost, Lewis.

Aggregates, Slates and Block Stone

Between Kyleakin and Broadford in Skye there occurs one of the largest deposits of sand and gravel in Scotland. It is composed of a wide variety of rock types, in a range of sizes, from boulders to sands and silts, the dominant rocks being quartzites and arkoses. The aggregates from this deposit were used for the making of high quality concrete, in the construction of oil-production platforms at the now defunct yard at Loch Kishorn. However, the deposits are of such great extent and high quality, that another market has been found. Efforts are being made to progressively rehabilitate the site as the aggregates are removed. At Sconser, fine-grained, grey Torridonian sandstone is quarried for concrete and lower grade road metals suitable for many of the secondary roads in Skye. The Torrin Quarry produces a high-grade limestone for rough casting and cladding panels (p. 62). It is also a good agricultural liming agent with a high magnesium content. Reserves are estimated at 0.75 million tonnes, but the limestone is cut by dykes and sills of dark dolerite and basalt, which lowers its value as a cladding material and creates much spoil.

At Ballygrant, in Islay, a dark marble in the Dalradian limestone is quarried and used as aggregate, agricultural lime and as block stone. The limestone island of Lismore possesses quarries and massive, long-disused lime kilns which produced agricultural lime for export to the peaty lands of Lorne and beyond. The kilns, buildings and harbour at Sailean are an industrial monument worthy of conservation. Similarly, the slate quarries of Easdale and Belnahua are monuments of a time of great industry in the Firth of Lorne. The complex of flooded quarry workings, industrial buildings and workers' cottages on Belnahua, set in a mosaic of islands, is a particularly deserving subject for conservation.

The greyish-pink granite of the Ross of Mull quarried near Bunessen makes high quality aggregates and building stone, well displayed in the Sherryvore Lighthouse and the shore station and dock at Hynish in Tiree (the latter is being restored by the Hebridean Trust). Near Rodel in South Harris, there is an emplacement of anorthosite which has a potential in the production of alumina, cement, and white roadstone.

Fisheries and Fish Farming chapter 5

Fishery History

The nature of the pristine Minches and the Sea of Hebrides may be reconstructed, in small part, from the organic deposits on the floors of the present-day submarine shelf. However, one fact is certain; the sea has always been held in highest reverence by the islanders, not only for its even-handed treatment of all men—whatever their rank—but also for its beneficence of food, fuel and fertiliser. What was once, though, an unexploited natural ecosystem of teeming life, probably of great variety, abundance and beauty now has waters that are subdued by a century and a half of mechanised fishing.

The Dutch were the first to fish the Minch commercially in the late 15th century, when the Loch Broom fishery was established (Darling, 1944), and by the early 18th century, the industry was booming in Tanera Mor and Isle Martin. The Dutch used herring busses which could reach off-shore waters, but, until then, the native fishermen used small communally-owned inshore boats, as their forebears had done. The aftermath of the Jacobite period brought English enterprise to the Highlands and Islands, which had a very limited effect on the life and economy of the local people. They were the work-force of the kelping industry, and generally too impoverished and subservient to be in any way commercially enterprising on their own behalf. However, with commercial enterprise from the south generally set on exploitation of both fisheries and people, there came to the Hebrides a commercially-minded philanthropist, one John Knox (no relation of the Calvinist reformer), a Scot by birth, and a wealthy bookseller in London. At the request of the British Fisheries Society (of which he was a prime-mover), Knox made a voyage to the north-west coast of Scotland in 1786, to survey and report on the prospects for fisheries. By his own account (1786), Knox's mission to the Hebrides was one of mercy along similar lines to Oxfam's present-day mission to the peoples of the Third World (Bray, 1986). Among other good works, he caused the British Fisheries Society to provide funds for the construction of small fishing villages of which Oban, Tobermory and

Ullapool are examples, and many other small quays, some of which were built by Thomas Telford.

Immediately following the collapse of kelping in the 1820s, the population was reaching its historical maximum in many islands and turned to fishing. Where this was financially supported by landowners in efforts to make estates economically viable, the industry became commercial, otherwise it continued at a local subsistence level to supplement agricultural crops. The end of the kelping brought great distress to island communities, poverty, and starvation; people often did not have the physical strength to man the heavy boats and the tackle required for a productive fishery, and were limited to clearing shell fish from the sea shore. However, about that time English companies were exporting salted herring to the West Indies as food for slaves.

The increasing population of the kelping period in the late 18th–early 19th centuries created hunger, which could only be relieved by a sufficiency of fish, particularly herring. Yet, prolific stocks were probably out of reach of many enfeebled communities. Fishing was by no means a ready-made form of subsistence for island communities; it was an uneasy tradition in many islands where the seafaring crafts, skills and traditions, for which Hebrideans later became noted in the British Mercantile Marine, were not in general practice. Lack of a ready native supply of timber for boats and the wild character of weather and sea were real drawbacks to organised fishing.

The new crofting system devised by landowners at that time to maintain the work force for kelping, depended for its survival on part-time fishing but nevertheless the inhabitants of the storm coasts of the island had few safe anchorages and little opportunity of sea-going. Islands like Eigg and Tiree, for example, had very limited shelter for a fishing fleet commensurate with their populations in the 1830s, and the opposite could be said for Canna and Eriskay.

The trauma of the potato famine in the 1840s and the continuous stream of emigrants also helped to bring about the capitalisation of the fishing industry. A deep-water herring fishery developed in the Minches, working to curing stations on the east coast of Lewis and Barra. The fishing industry of the islands had mushroomed from being one of local subsistence fishing in the 17th century, to being in the 19th century one of general sufficiency throughout the Hebrides as a whole, supporting a flourishing export trade, particularly in barrel-cured herring.

The fortunes of the island communities in the 19th century were dependent on the herring industry; more than any other fish, the herring epitomised the marine harvest, which

promised to be the supplement of agriculture and a basis for livelihood. Until about 1914, the herring, the six-eared oat, and the potato made the islands habitable by large numbers of people living a simple life. There is a history of herring fishing at Stornoway, and the remains of herring stations are found also at Castlebay, the Summer Isles and Badcall, and many landing quays, of which Canna was a good example, were used between 1892 and 1905. The advent of the railheads and the replacement of sail by steam in the drifters caused a rapid decline of the local quay industry, with the focus of landings moved to market ports such as Stornoway, Mallaig, and Oban with fast rail and sea services.

The small fishing harbour at Port of Ness, Lewis in 1976 (Photo J. M. Boyd)

The seasonal nature of the herring fishery fitted well with the timing of agricultural work. Herring shoals in the sheltered sea lochs in winter, and in the more exposed off-shore waters in summer, attracted fleets of boats with drift nets when times were slack on the crofts. However, shoaling from year to year was uncertain, and the main stocks of herring occurred annually in the west coast before they appeared on the east coast. This provided an employment incentive which transformed life in many crofter-fisher communities in the Hebrides. Both men and women left home in large numbers to seek jobs at fishing ports from Shetland to Yarmouth; men found places in east coast drifter crews and women on the curing lines at the harbours. Fishing had become an almost year-round occupation and, though many returned to maintain their crofts in season, others did not and the general level of agricultural efficiency declined. In 1884, the Napier Commission believed that more income came into crofting from the sea than from the land, and by 1891, the Walpole Commission claimed that three out of four people in the Highlands and Islands were in some way dependent on fishing for their livelihood. In 1902 the Brand Report stated that the average family in Lewis drew an annual income of £3 from the sale of croft produce, and £25 from fishing (Smout, 1986).

The replacement of sail by steam brought a new power to the fishing industry of the late 19th century, both in main propulsion engines, and in windlasses for hauling nets and lines. The large scale mechanical exploitation of the continental-shelf fishery had begun, in which home-based boats played only a minor part. Hebridean waters were worked by succeeding generations of steam trawlers and drifters, with an increasing use of ice to chill the catches of white fish bound for distant ports, such as Fleetwood and Aberdeen. A vast amount of the herring catch at the beginning of this century was exported by klondikers to Russia, but the advent of the First World War and the Russian Revolution destroyed this market, and the herring industry collapsed. It was at this time that Lord Leverhulme built the fishing stations at Leverburgh, Harris and Carloway, Lewis, in an attempt to revitalise the fishing industry.

The Leverhulme enterprise, 1918–25, was based on the herring. However, the vision of the marine harvest conveyed

Mallaig harbour in the 1960s showing herring drifters and fishermen drawing the drift nets. Now this harbour is busy with purse-seiners, small trawlers and creelers (Photo J. M. Boyd)

through investment and business acumen to the consumer society of industrial Britain depended on more than the abundance of herring; it depended also on the outright support of the Lewismen, which was not provided. Leverhulme moved to Harris in 1924 but died in 1925, thus ending a fine scheme which might have been of enduring benefit to the Hebrides and Gaelic culture. The fishing harbours at Carloway and Leverburgh remain as monuments to a great idea.

The growth of the industry in the late 19th–early 20th centuries was also marked by the rise in importance of landings at Canna and later at the railhead ports of Kyle of Lochalsh, Mallaig and Oban. Boats from Campbeltown and Tarbert on Loch Fyne fished waters around the southern Hebrides and shipped their catches to Clyde ports by fast cargo/passenger steamers. The old fish-curing stations on the coasts of Ross and Cromarty and Sutherland were replaced by other larger harbours close to good fishing grounds in the North Minch at Ullapool, Lochinver and Kinlochbervie.

Though the two World Wars disrupted the industry, they also served to stimulate new efforts to rebuild the fishing fleets operating in the Hebrides for part of the year. The steam-powered vessels declined between the wars and were totally eclipsed in the second half of this century by diesel vessels with sophisticated electrical, and electronic equipment—trawlers, pair trawlers, ringers and purse-seiners. Costs soared, the numbers of boats decreased, many fewer men were required in mechanised fishing, and the catching power of the boats increased many fold. Trawlers and lobster smacks from the Netherlands, Spain and France and long-liners from Scandinavia have joined the British fleets in the fishery bonanza of the last century. Today, a large mackerel fishery still persists in the North Minch based on Loch Broom, with much smaller quantities of herring landed there and at Stornoway and Campbeltown (Table 3). A sizeable trade in white fish is still carried out at Oban, Mallaig, Lochinver and Kinlochbervie. The fish-processing plant at Stornoway has been supplemented in recent years by others, at Breasclete in Lewis and Ardveenish in Barra, ostensibly to exploit the stocks of blue whiting on the continental slope west and north of the Outer Hebrides. The former is being redeployed to the making of chemical extracts from fish oil, and the latter has had an erratic employment record. Grants are available for vessels to supply these and other plants, but most local investment has gone into the provision of small two-man craft equipped for creeling, trawling, or dredging for shellfish.

In recent years, mackerel have been fished by Scottish and foreign purse-seiners supplying a pack of eastern European factory ships anchored in Loch Broom, and the fish-meal factory at Stornoway. The Minch fishery has now nearly ended. It is claimed that this is due to a redistribution of the stocks, but the visual impact of the fleet of ships off Ullapool, which are now siphoning off mackerel from waters further to the north, suggests over-exploitation of the mackerel stocks and points to a need for restrictions now, or in the near future. Catch quotas have already been recommended. The only commercial profit to the local economy from this fishing activity is in the supply of some services.

The main industrial fisheries presently in the Hebrides are the ones for sand-eels in the areas of the north Minch, North Rona and sometimes off Barra, for Norway pout southwest of Barra (which is exploited by the Danes and Faroese), and for blue whiting along the shelf edge west of St Kilda. Industrial fishing may, however, also threaten the stocks of mackerel and sprat. All these species are of importance to the stability of the marine ecosytem and the future of many other dependent species. Some species, like herring, have been substantially exploited yet still survive. Sadly, this is more a reflection of the enormous reproductive powers of the species than of the foresight of fisheries managers. The mackerel may be a different story again, but there is little doubt that our view of the seas as an ever-bountiful source of protein is highly misconceived. Today, fisheries management proceeds by trial and error. This is partly because we are not yet sophisticated enough to understand the complex population and community dynamics of fish, but it is also because it is politically expedient to proceed in this manner. This approach leads to short-term industrial boom instead of long-term stability and there are a remarkable number of people still willing to support the boom or bust approach.

Both fishing stations are within easy reach of fish stock around St Kilda, the prime seabird breeding station in the British Isles and the first natural site in the United Kingdom to be included in the World Heritage Convention (WHC). In this it joins the Gallapagos, Aldabra and Tristan da Cunha. We do not know if industrial fishing poses a threat to the seabirds, but evidence from Shetland points to this.

Demersal and Pelagic Fish

The most important species of demersal or bottom-feeding species fished in Hebridean waters are cod (*Gadus morhua*), haddock (*Melanogrammus aeglefinus*), whiting (*Merlangius mer-*

langius) and spurdogs (*Squalus acanthias*). Saithe (*Pollachius virens*), hake (*Merluccius merluccius*), ling (*Molva molva*), skate (*Rajidae*), angler fish (*Lophius piscatorius*) and plaice (*Pleuronectes platessa*) are less abundant. (Biological aspects of these species, and of the pelagic species and shellfish mentioned below, are discussed in Chapter 4, H-ANT).

The blue whiting (Micromesistius poutassou) (Crown Copyright)

Turning to the pelagic or surface-feeding species, herring (*Clupea harengus*) are by far the most important. The history of herring landings in the Stornoway District (Outer Hebrides) are shown in Table 3. Until 1935, the catches of herring showed large-scale annual fluctuations between 5,000 and 45,000 tonnes, but after 1935 these catches fluctuated on a distinctly lower plane of between 3,000 and 17,000 tonnes, with a marked upsurge about 1970 when the purse seine net was introduced. Mackerel (*Scomber scomber*) was traditionally only a minor part of the pelagic fishery (*c.* 1,000 tonnes annually) and sprats (*Spratus spratus*) began to be commercially fished in the early 1970s, when 'industrial' fishing began, and there was also an increase in the mackerel catch to support the fish-processing industry. In recent years the 'industrial' fishery has been extended to include the demersal Norway pout (*Trisopterus esmarkii*), the sand-eel (*Ammodytes* spp.) and blue whiting (*Micromesistius poutassou*) (Table 1).

The harvest of 'industrial' fish supplies fish meal for agriculture and aquaculture in the United Kingdom. This meal is processed from whole 'industrial' species and the waste products of the white fish, herring and mackerel industries. A recent survey by G. M. Bishop (1987) shows that the annual national need for fish meal is about 300,000 tonnes, of which 71,000t (24%) is obtained from a harvest of about 350,000t of raw fish from home waters—the remaining 76% is imported. In 1987, the requirement of British aquaculture for fish meal (which constitutes about 55% of the food of farmed fish) was about 21,000t, obtained from about 100,000t of raw fish. Quantities of this catch are taken on the Hebridean shelf and landed at Stornoway and Mallaig (Table 1). These quantities are not large in relation to the standing stock of these species present in Hebridean waters, but the increase in the catch of sand-eels in the Outer Hebrides is very significant. From zero in 1976, the catch in 1986 had grown to 24,376t valued at £675,600.

Year	Stornoway			Mallaig		
	N.pout	S.eel	Bl.whg	N.pout	S.eel	Bl.whg
1976	6,319		817	26		382
1977	2,853	13	1,291	37	190	1,289
1978	302		498	29	192	1,073
1979	19		1,464	28	215	
1980	1,202	212	4,098			
1981	1,158	5,972	2,391			
1982	585	10,872				
1983		12,882				
1984	23	12,359				
1985	13	18,586				
1986		24,376	4,028			

Table 1 The weights (tonnes) of Norway pout, sand-eels and blue whiting landed at Stornoway and Mallaig 1976–86 (*Sea Fishery Statistical Tables 1976–86*) N. pout=Norway pout, bl Whg=blue whiting.

Sand-eels are not part of the European diet; the same fish in Third World countries would be a staple food. There is an overriding principle at work here, namely, that a vast quantity of low-cost fish which is wholesome food for all people is exploited in the creation of a small quantity of high-cost food for a few people.

Pelagic fish (85% mackerel) landed from the Minch at Ulla-pool have increased enormously (Table 3). In 1976, 7,492t of mackerel valued at £0.40 million were landed at Ullapool compared with 177,916t valued at £19.65 million in 1985. This is a 24-fold increase in the take from the stock in the Minch in a decade—surely such exploitation is well beyond the limits of rational conservation of mackerel stocks?

Shellfish

The shellfish industry is based on stocks of lobsters (*Homarus vulgaris*) and Norway lobsters (*Nephrops norvegicus*), with lesser fisheries of scallops (*Pecten maximus*), crabs (*Cancer pagurus*), periwinkles (*Littorina littorea*), and cockles (*Cerastoderma edule*).

Since the last war the shellfish industry, traditionally a creel fishery for lobsters by crofter-fishermen, has become more highly mechanised with larger well-equipped creelers for lobsters and crabs, trawlers and creelers for *Nephrops*, and dredgers for scallops and clams. Catches are marketed at main ports for freezing, though catches are sometimes also kept alive in holding ponds awaiting suitable market conditions. Consequently, high quality fresh shellfish are sent to the market or direct to the consumer by air. The changing palate of the British people and considerable exports have made *Nephrops* the most profitable shellfish.

In 1952, the value of the landings of shellfish in Scotland was £296,000; in 1976, it was £12,384,000, when the landings in the Outer Hebrides reached their highest ever value, £1,046,000. In the Inner Hebrides, landings decreased from 1971 when there was a peak in lobster landings of 150t. Until then large creelers working the prolific grounds to the west of the Outer Hebrides landed their catches at Mallaig. However, increasing costs of fuel in the early 1970s forced these boats to land catches in the Outer Hebrides. This contributed to the peak landing in 1976 in the Outer Isles, when that in the Inner Isles was much reduced, resulting in the closure of the lobster-holding tanks in Mallaig. By 1986, only 56t were landed at Mallaig and Oban Fishery Districts, compared with 129t in the Stornoway District (Table 2).

Mason *et al.* (1983) state that the shift of landings from Mallaig to the Outer Hebrides is only part of the reason for the decline of the fishery in the Inner Hebrides. The lobster population has undoubtedly decreased and the decline in the catch of lobsters per unit of catching effort in the 1970s in the Inner Hebrides is deemed typical of the entire west coast fishery in that period. The fishing effort in the past 25 years has been greater than that which would result in a maximum sustainable yield, and the situation has not improved in the 1980s. Paradoxically, while the catch of lobsters has declined, the value of that catch increased greatly until the late 1970s, when the price dropped as North American lobsters claimed a substantial hold on the European market.

The Norway lobster is a burrow-dweller, which until the early 1950s, was taken accidentally by trawlers seeking white fish. Thereafter, a market was sought for this species, and within ten years it had become a major fishery working to an expanding seafood processing industry. From 100t in 1953, the size of the Scottish *Nephrops* catch in 1985 had grown to 17,887t, valued at £24,275,000, and between 1976 to 1986, the catch of *Nephrops* in the five Fishery Districts of the Hebrides (Table 4) increased from 5,833t valued at £3.47 million to 9,222t

	Strny	Kilbre	Lhnvr	Ullpl	Mallg	Oban	Cpbtn
Demersal Fish							
Cod	135	1,543	468	36	556	45	168
Dogfish	143	697	715	15	576	120	144
Haddock	371	7,371	2,602	110	1,509	268	15
Hake	30	39	75	2	160	117	117
Halibut	2	13	7	<1	3	<1	<1
Monkfish	107	248	204	4	314	18	7
Plaice	33	325	329	3	66	52	14
Saithe	9	1,432	73	2	169	1	55
Skate	56	508	494	32	241	123	26
Whiting	170	2,877	1,003	18	841	376	68
Totals	1,056	15,053	5,970	223	4,436	1,121	615
Pelagic Fish							
Herring	2,301			18,077	457		736
Mackerel	1,481			101,527	561		92
Bl.whit.	4,028						
Sprats	74				238		209
S.eels*	24,376				<1		
Totals	32,260			119,594	1,257		1,037
Shellfish							
Pwinkles	225			47	491	227	145
Crabs	805	3	34	71	95	108	230
Lobsters	129	13	3	5	17	39	34
Scallops	489		2	133	456	814	693
N.lobsters	1,242	4	890	868	3,177	780	2,261
Squid	<1	203	237	4	60	3	1
Qu.scallops					10	71	158
Totals	2,891	223	1,166	1,128	4,306	2,042	34,221

*The sand-eel is a demersal species but is included in the list of pelagic fish because of its industrial use similar to other pelagic species.

Table 2 Landings (tonnes) of the main species of finfish and shellfish by British vessels in the Fishery Districts of Stornoway (Strny), Kinlochbervie (Klbre), Lochinver (Lhnvr), Ullapool (Ullpl), Mallaig (Mallg), Oban and Campbeltown (Cpbtn), in 1986 (*Scottish Sea Fisheries Statistical Tables, 1986*).

valued at £16.30 million. Again the question arises—is such a high level of exploitation in the interests of the long term conservation of stocks?

We have reviewed the history of the Hebridean fishery in some detail, since only by doing so can we convey the enormous change that man has made to the marine environment of the Hebrides—and over the Continental Shelf as a whole. This impact takes several forms; there is the direct impact of

District	Weight (tonnes)					Value (£'000)				
	1982	1983	1984	1985	1986	1982	1983	1984	1985	1986
Demersal Fish										
Strny	13,192	14,733	13,980	20,079	25,597	829	990	1,018	1,147	1,385
Klbre	n/a	n/a	17,753	18,984	15,601	n/a	n/a	10,074	10,433	9,490
Lhnvr	n/a	n/a	n/a	n/a	6,510	n/a	n/a	n/a	n/a	4,088
Ullpl	17,620	17,323	8,525	6,786	244	7,003	8,080	4,109	3,968	126
Mallg	3,925	5,311	6,640	6,911	4,956	1,337	2,376	3,289	4,031	3,581
Oban	3,452	3,987	2,870	2,201	1,190	1,286	1,756	1,485	1,138	820
Cpbtn	928	870	663	974	643	320	279	235	411	442
Totals	39,117	42,224	50,431	55,935	54,741	10,775	13,481	20,210	21,128	19,932
Scotland	296,245	292,874	282,749	294,739	281,758	106,444	121,102	135,997	147,153	163,050
Pelagic Fish										
Strny	11,802	6,811	6,887	8,942	7,928	496	3,882	418	477	283
Klbre	n/a	n/a				n/a	n/a			
Lhnvr	n/a	n/a	n/a	n/a		n/a	n/a	n/a	n/a	
Ullpl	140,191	139,880	173,708	177,916	119,603	15,321	15,841	18,165	19,651	12,660
Mallg	3,681	3,001	852	1,875	1,256	449	414	91	169	135
Oban		54	181	132			7	25	15	
Cpbtn	1,572	2,070	1,974	1,947	1,037	354	380	370	412	289
Totals	157,246	151,816	183,602	190,812	129,824	16,620	17,524	19,069	20,724	13,367
Scotland	172,916	173,560	226,020	263,099	234,707	18,510	19,929	24,445	28,974	25,370
Shellfish										
Strny	2,558	3,145	3,826	4,095	3,108	2,117	3,082	4,128	5,103	4,568
Klbre	n/a	n/a	156	134	224	n/a	n/a	349	315	432
Lhnvr	n/a	n/a	n/a	n/a	1,165	n/a	n/a	n/a	n/a	2,055
Ullpl	2,217	2,046	2,536	2,200	1,127	2,601	2,640	2,935	2,919	1,835
Mallg	4,330	3,991	5,085	4,725	4,384	4,427	4,084	5,484	6,159	7,066
Oban	2,524	2,372	2,307	1,955	2,177	2,068	2,037	2,371	2,394	3,210
Cpbtn	4,193	4,471	4,308	4,133	3,813	3,339	4,095	4,705	4,801	5,965
Totals	16,822	12,880	14,236	13,013	11,501	12,435	12,856	15,495	16,273	18,076
Scotland	29,027	32,713	34,543	34,732	34,798	23,754	29,183	33,477	38,976	46,030

Table 3   Weights and values of landings of finfish and shellfish by British vessels in the Fishery Districts of Stornoway (Strny), Kinlochbervie (Klbre), Lochinver (Lhnvr), Ullapool (Ullpl), Mallaig (Mallg), Oban and Campbeltown (Cpbtn), in the period 1977–86 (*Scottish Sea Fisheries Statistical Tables, 1986*).

the quarry species and the consequent changes in their numerical status; the impact on the non-quarry species which are taken accidentally; also, small or young classes of some species are taken while fishing for adult forms of small quarry species such as sprats, sand-eels, *Nephrops* and clams. Gravid females are caught and, perhaps most important of all, there is a physical impact on the sea-bed caused by frequent passes of trawlers and dredgers over the limited sheets of mud in quest of *Nephrops*, sand and gravels for scallops, and the scarifying of wide areas by trawlers for benthic finfish. No holistic forethought has ever been given to the consequence of this disturbance of the Hebridean shelf; the sea-bed has been created by nature in 10,000 years and has been substantially impoverished by man in the last 100.

District	1976		1986	
	t	£	t	£
Stornoway	978	489,155	1,242	2,017,700
Kinlochbervie			4	7,500
Lochinver			890	1,565,700
Ullapool	1,019	662,666	3,177	1,595,100
Mallaig	2,417	1,529,864	3,177	5,964,500
Oban	650	370,380	780	1,338,300
Campbeltown	769	417,108	2,261	3,810,000
Totals	5,833	3,469,173	9,222	16,298,800

Table 4   A comparison of the weights (tonnes) and value of landings of Norway lobsters (*Nephrops norvegicus*) in the five Fishery Districts covering Hebridean waters, in 1976 and 1986 (*Scottish Sea Fisheries Statistical Tables, 1976 and 1986*).

Fish Farming

The rapid growth of fish farming on the western and northern seaboards of Scotland came at a time of great effort to create employment in crofting areas. In the 1980s, fishfarming has provided a complement to the agricultural revival under the IDP (see p. 51) in the Outer Hebrides and the Agricultural Development Programme (ADP) in the Inner Hebrides; it now has an almost open-ended potential for development. As if by magic, all the factors — technical, ecological and social — were right for the attraction of venture capital, and the growth of an industry which was, in many respects, compatible with the Highlands and Islands. Looking at the setting of the industry, the length of suitable coastline for farms seems enormous; the volume of clean seawater available for exchange with the ocean reservoir limitless; supplies of processed fish food inexhaustible; and the appetite of affluent people all over the world for 'Scotch' salmon insatiable. The opportunities for development seem to be near to ideal, but are they? Supplies of 'industrial' fish (see p. 70) which form a large part of processed fish food, are indeed exhaustible in the commercial sense, and any serious widespread pollution along the seaboard brings to question the cleanliness of the sea water and the quality of the fish for sensitive markets. The biological and engineering problems are formidable, and the harvest is at constant risk of damage and destruction by storm and disease.

The farmed 'Scotch' salmon is the indigenous Atlantic salmon (*Salmo salar*). The freshwater phase of the production cycle covers the egg, fry, parr and smolt stages; the marine phase covers the grilse and salmon growth stages. Brood adults in farms are stripped of their eggs which are fertilised and set in trays in running freshwater. Fry and parr are brought on to feeding in tanks and, when a few grams in weight, are transferred to freshwater tanks or cages in freshwater lochs, where they grow for one or two years until they become smolts. The bulk of the parr stock become 'silvered' after one year and is transferred as smolts into seawater cages. Here they are grown for one year to be harvested as grilse (1.5–2.0kg), or 18 months as salmon (2.0–4.0kg). Other smolts are either kept for another year or are disposed of, sometimes by release into the sea or river. The grilse are the fish which show signs of coming early into breeding condition and thus dropping in market value the longer they are retained. The bulk of the harvest (*c.* 70%) goes to market as salmon, and selected fish are retained as brood stock. There is also a thriving market for salmon ova stripped from wild-caught fish from the rivers.

Rainbow trout (*Salmo gairdneri*) and native brown trout (*Salmo trutta*) are both farmed on a small scale in the Hebrides, mainly as 'portion-sized' fish for the catering trade, and the latter also to a minor extent for the stocking of angling waters. The production cycle is again six months for the egg, fry and fingerling stages in freshwater tanks, followed by another six or twelve months growth in larger tanks, ponds, freshwater or sea cages. The trout are harvested when between 280 and 340gms in weight.

Mussels (*Mytilus edulis*), clams (*Pecten maximus*), queen scallops (*Chlamys opercularis*), the native oyster (*Ostrea edulis*) and the Pacific oyster (*Crassostrea gigas*) are farmed in the Hebrides. The mussels are grown to market-size in 18 months from natural spat collected on suspended ropes. Sometimes the spat is collected in one area and grown in another. The scallops are grown to market-size over a period of about three years from natural spat, which, having been collected from the sea bed, is transferred to suspended nets; alternatively the shells may be drilled and the scallop suspended individually in the 'pierced-ear culture'. The Pacific oysters are grown to market-size in 18 months from hatchery-produced spat in net bags suspended just above the sea bed.

Fish farming, therefore, is a new, major, widespread, ecological factor suddenly imposed upon the coastal environment of north-west Scotland in advance of a thorough knowledge of the marine ecology. The flora and fauna, and the processes which govern life on land and the sea-shore, are far more scrutible, and much better known and understood, than those in the sea. Indeed, the nature of the sea being basically different from that of the land, the ecological rationale of the land cannot be simply extended to the marine realm. The water column of the sea is a vast, dense, mobile, environment in its own right, related to, but in many respects separate from, the sea-bed. The relationships between the sea and the sea-bed are poorly understood, and it is within this area of uncertainty, that the fish farming industry is placed.

The uncertainty created by a lack of scientific knowledge was accompanied by a lack of statutory planning regulations for the off-shore side of the industry. The Crown Estate Commission (CEC) is legally responsible for leases of the sea-bed to fish farmers. Concern about the environmental aspects of the off-shore installations was expressed by both development and conservation bodies, which has resulted in published reports by Cobham Resource Consultants (1987), Gowen, *et al.* (1988), Scottish Wildlife and Countryside Link (SWCL) (1988), and the NCC (1989).

The immediate and short-term effects of fish farms on the environment are local, and in most cases predictable. On land the effects are subject to statutory planning control by the local authority, who can call for an environmental impact assessment. Off-shore, there is no such control, only the conditions accompanying the lease of the seabed by the CEC, which has potentially conflicting interests — the raising of revenues from such leases, as well as care for the environment. The CEC has published *Guidelines on Siting and Design of Marine Fish Farms in Scotland* (1987) and has co-operated with the HIDB, CCS, NCC and the Scottish Salmon Growers' Association in sponsoring of the first two of the above reports. Those moves show that the CEC are determined to fully address their responsibilities. However, a question remains over the propriety of a financially-interested body, (no matter how well-intended) acting in the public interest in a matter of such scale and importance as fish farming. The third report was sponsored by twelve non-government conservation bodies. The scale of public reaction to the fish-farming bonanza, therefore, is great, timely, and directed towards closing gaps in science, planning and administration.

The impacts of salmon and trout farms are much greater than those of shellfish farms, because shellfish take natural, planktonic food from the sea, whereas salmon and trout in farms depend on pelleted food. The long-term effects of various forms of pollution and chemical additives to encourage growth of fish, to combat disease and parasitism of fish, and to reduce the fouling, rotting and corrosion of nets and cages, are much less predictable. Clearly, such long-term effects are dependent on the size and number of farms and the rate of tidal flushing of the moorings. In turn, the density of farms may be limited by the need to keep well apart different stocks of fish possessing differing origins and health records and also by the development of more robust cages making it possible to extend farming into waters which previously were too exposed.

When salmon cages are first established the water column and seabed beneath the salmon cages becomes gradually polluted by the faeces and unconsumed food of the salmon. It takes up to six months for the seabed to reach a new ecological state, sustained by the continuous loading of the seabed with wastes, which accumulate at 2–7kgm per sq m per year. In still waters, systems can become unstable, due to the growth of phytoplankton, and in summer sunshine heavy loadings of soluble nitrogen derived from organic decomposition and faeces may cause a 'bloom' of phytoplankton. Some 'blooms', in turn, contain toxins, deoxygenate the water column and pose a serious threat to the fish stock. Salmon stocks in the sea can also be affected by algal blooms. In warm, calm spells of several weeks with long periods of sunshine, as occur in north-west Scotland at intervals of a few years, a thermocline can develop in the sheltered waters of the sea lochs. The water above the thermocline becomes enriched both naturally and by wastes from the fish farm, and a bloom can develop with toxic and anoxic conditions, which will quickly kill caged stocks of salmon. Such a die-off occurred in Loch Torridon in 1988. In freshwaters an increased supply of phosphorus can trigger blooms which may seriously affect caged smolt and trout stocks.

The natural community of the seabed, which is greatly varied and is symptomatic of stable healthy conditions, is partially or totally replaced by another community, accompanied by 'gassing'—a decline of oxygen accompanied by an increase of methane and hydrogen sulphide. Gassing, of course, can have an adverse effect on the farmed fish, and care must be taken with cages sited in shallow areas with a slow exchange of water. The replacement community is less varied than the natural, and is described in detail by Gowen *et al.* for a salmon farm in Loch Spelve, Mull, and by Earll *et al.* for farms in the Outer Hebrides. The survey in Loch Spelve has given information on the effects of the fish farm on the entire loch, and shows how the effects rapidly fall-off with distance from the farm. Effects were localised, and over 150m from the cages the community was natural to the loch. The benthic fauna beneath salmon cages was dominated (sometimes 100%) by the opportunistic polychaetes, *Capitella capitata* and *Scololepis fuliginosa*. Beneath the rafts of mussel farms in the Outer Hebrides, starfish (*Asterias rubens*) and shore crabs (*Carcinus maenas*) seem to tolerate some anoxic regimes, feed off the invertebrate fauna (of which there may be over 100 species) and faeces which become dislodged from the mussel ropes. At moorings with a good tidal exchange, shoals of saithe (*Pollachius virens*) and schools of other in-shore fish congregate to feed on the fall-out from the cages and rafts, and the activities of all these scavengers in the sea bed and water column help to dissipate the concentrations of organic waste. Such conditions occur naturally in many dumps of rotting organic material with the production of much toxic gas. Dead seaweed stagnates in still 'sinks' in sheltered inlets, and the bacterium *Beggiatoa* grows in ghostly white sheets over the decaying weed as it also does beneath some cages and rafts. It is a sure indicator of anoxic conditions — though to thrive, it requires both methane and oxygen; the former it obtains from the sediments and the latter from the seawater.

The effect of fish farms on the seabed is rapid, but depends on the rate of water exchange and the scale of farming. Three months from the start of a typical salmon farm, the sediments beneath the cages are anoxic, and the pollution-tolerant polychaetes become dominant. In six months, the 'pollution' community and the gradient of the community outwards from the farm is established. The recovery of the seabed from fish farming can be rapid, however. The organic wastes are mobilised and gradually dissipated within the sediments, and the natural benthic community reoccupies the site, but not exactly in the same form as before the farm was begun. Gowen *et al.* (1988) state that after six months use, sediments took three months to regain the natural state, but the fauna remained dominated by a 'pollution' fauna, while after three years continuous use, the sediments took eight months to revert, but the 'pollution' fauna dominated beyond that time.

Observations have of necessity been taken from farms of less than twenty years standing, placed in otherwise unfarmed seas. The recovery of a disused site in a sheltered sea loch, which has had a heavy complement of farms for a century, may be different. The long-term effects of continuous use of sheltered sealochs and inlets for salmon farming, where there is limited exchange of seawater and many natural 'sinks', cannot be easily predicted from examination of the short-term effects. In this book we are dealing with the scientific aspects, but the scenic and amenity aspects are of no less importance and are closely related to our ecological account.

Salmon farming has been superimposed upon the natural population of *Salmo salar* breeding in Scottish rivers and feeding in the North Atlantic. Farmed salmon stocks tend to be selected for placid behaviour, late sexual development and fast growth to a standard marketable type. Large numbers of parr which do not develop into smolts in one year are often released

into the wild, and this accidental or deliberate release of
farmed fish over decades may pose a threat to the genetic
make-up of wild salmon (Maitland, 1987).

Genetic effects are another largely unknown sector of
salmon farming, which requires urgent research and is closely
related to the control of diseases. The levels of immunity of
different stocks of fish to different viruses, bacteria and fungae
is likely to vary between farmed stocks and between farmed and
wild fish. For example, Norwegian and Scottish stocks farmed
in the same sea loch may be immune to their own but vulnerable to each other's pathogens. In 1986, of the 38.6 million eggs
used by the industry, 1.7 million (4.4%) were from 'Norwegian
sources' (SWCL, 1988), and in the last decade, the ecto-
parasitic fluke (*Gyrodactylus salaris*) has spread from farmed
parr to wild salmon in Norwegian rivers. Entire rivers have had
to be cleared of salmon at enormous financial and ecological
cost, in efforts to eradicate the parasite. The infections are
thought to have been caused by the import of infected fish from
one or more of 28 watercourses and 11 hatcheries that hold the

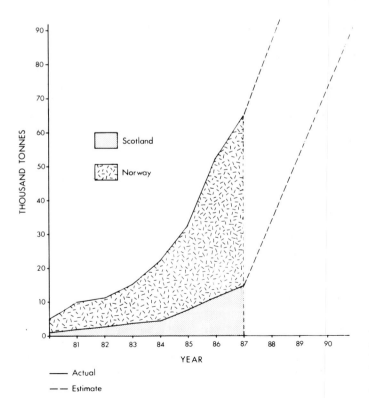

Fig. 53
*Production of Atlantic
farmed salmon in
Scotland and Norway
1980–1987 (Nature
Conservancy Council,
1989)*

parasite. The ecological effects of the introduction of large numbers of alien smolts into the runs of wild salmon are also unknown, and little or no allowance is made for the possible disruption of the migratory processes of native fish.

The fish farms occur within the long established ranges of wild predators of fish, and are a great attraction to them. Cormorant (*Phalacrocorax carbo*), shags (*P. aristotelis*), heron (*Ardea cinerea*), common seal (*Phoca vitulina*), grey seals (*Halichoerus grypus*), otter (*Lutra lutra*) and feral mink (*Mustela vison*) are the predators of salmon and trout farms, while mussel

Fig. 6
*Location of fish farms in the Hebrides
(Nature Conservancy Council, 1989)*

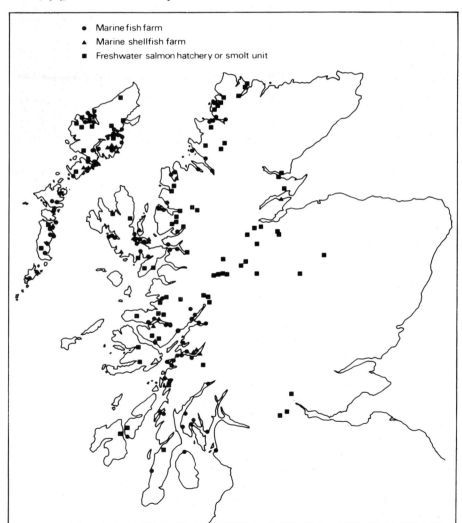

- ● Marine fish farm
- ▲ Marine shellfish farm
- ■ Freshwater salmon hatchery or smolt unit

farms are vulnerable to eiders (*Somateria mollissima*). Fish stocks are defended by the netting of cages, scaring devices, trapping, poisoning and shooting. The powerful effect that these attractions have on the natural instincts of these predators in their native habitat, coupled with their continuous destruction, has caused much controversy. Fortunately, all of these species have an ample food supply in the Hebrides. However, salmon farms in close proximity to a cormorant colony such as that at Loch an Tomain in North Uist, or to the otter shores at Kylerhea, Skye, and Loch Scridain in Mull, or the seal rocks in the Firth of Lorne and Colonsay, are likely to pose problems in predator control, as would mussel farms near eider islands at Kyleakin in Skye. A presumption against the siting of fish farms within 8km of major, long-established assemblies of protected birds, otters and seals could avoid constant harassment of farms, and the killing of the predators.

Fish farming in Loch Ainort, Skye (Photo R. E. Garner)

    With a few exceptions, trout farming is a mainland occupation, while salmon and shellfish farms are concentrated on the western seaboard, the Hebrides, Orkney and Shetland (Fig. 6). Table 5 shows the numbers of fish farms in the Hebrides in 1986, but these figures have changed rapidly upwards, since several hundred applications for leases in Scotland have been approved by the Crown Estate Commissioners (CEC) who administer the seabed. At least 250 applications for such leases were made in 1987 (SCWL, 1988).

Island	Salmon in freshwater	Salmon in sea water	Trout	Shellfish	Totals
Lewis	5	20	6	13	44
Harris	2	6		7	15
North Uist		4		3	7
Benbecula		1		5	6
South Uist	1	8		6	15
Barra		3		3	6
Out.Hebrides	8	42	6	37	93
Summer Isles		1			1
Raasay					
Skye	2	8	1	6	17
Small Isles					
Tiree					
Coll					
Mull	1	3	1	4	9
Jura		1			1
Islay				1	1
Colonsay				1	1
Kerrera		1		3	4
Gigha		1		1	2
Inn.Hebrides	3	15	2	16	36
Hebrides	11	57	8	53	129
Scotland	66	127	73	150	416

Table 5 Numbers of fish farms in the Hebrides in 1986—compiled from *Marine Fishfarming in Scotland* (Scottish Wildlife and Countryside Link, 1988) and *An Environmental Assessment of Fish Farms* (Countryside Commission for Scotland *et al.*).

The widespread, open-ended potential of fish farming in the Highlands and Islands generates hope for industrial development and employment, however, to a public that is now more aware than ever before of the need for environmental care, it also generates caution, about how far and how fast it can be taken without damage to scenery, wildlife, other human interests and ultimately to itself.

Fig. 5 shows the scale of salmon farming in Scotland and Norway. The strong competition between the two industries for markets can be adjudged.

Nature Conservation

Conservation of nature is a culture of the twentieth century possessing its own philosophical, ethical and scientific frame, distinct from those of agriculture, fisheries and forestry. It is directed towards the maintenance of numbers of different species, distributed in different habitats of natural or semi-natural type, and towards the care of geological and physiographical features. It also requires the disciplining of nature, as in the control of aggressive, colonising species, but such action is usually on a local or limited scale. There has been little of such management in the Hebrides, largely because the need has not arisen; it has not been necessary to turn back the tide of development by preserving small islands of habitat in the midst of urban or agricultural lands, nor has conservation been involved to any great degree in revitalising countryside devastated by pesticides, fertilisers, drainage or general unsympathetic

A geological SSSI on Kerrera—lower Old Red Sandstone conglomerate lies unconformably over folded slates and limestone (Photo British Geological Survey)

Figure 7 *a* & *b* Map
showing the distribution
of Sites of Special
Scientific Interest in the
Hebrides, indicating
those of biological,
geological, and 'mixed'
interest (updated from
Boyd, 1979 and Boyd
and Kerr, 1983).
Fig. 55*a*: Outer
Hebrides and Skye
1. Achmore Bog 2. Allt
Volagir, 3. Baleshare
and Kirkibost,
4. Balranald Bog and
Loch nam Feithean,
5. Bornish and
Ormiclate Machair,
6. Eoligarry, 7. Flannan
Islands, 8. Glen
Valtos 9. Gress
Saltings, 10. Howmore
Estuary, 11. Little Loch
Roag Valley Bog,
12. Loch a' Sgurr
Pegmatite, 13. Loch an
Duin, 14. Loch Bee,
15. Loch Dalbeg,
16. Loch Druidibeg,
17. Loch Hallan Fens,
18. Lochs Laxavat Ard
and Iorach, 19. Loch
Meurach, 20. Loch na
Cartach, 21. Loch nan
Eilean Valley Bog,
22. Loch Obisary,
23. Loch Orasay,
24. Loch Scadavay,
25. Loch Scarrasdale
Bog, 26. Loch
Stiapavat, 27. Loch
Tuamister, 28. Lochs
at Clachan,
29. Luskentyre Banks
and Saltings,
30. Machairs Robach
and Newton,
31. Mangersta Sands,
32. Mingulay and
Berneray, 33. Monach
Isles, 34. North Harris,
35. North Rona and Sula
Sgeir, 36. Northton Bay,
37. Rockall, 38. Shiant
Isles, 39. Small Seal
Islands, 40. St Kilda,
41. Stornoway Castle
Woods, 42. Tolsta
Head, 43. Tong
Saltings, 44. West
Lochs, 45. Aird
Thuirinis—Port na
Long, 46. Airdghunail,
47. Allt Geodh a
Ghamhna, 48. Allt
Grillan Gorge, 49. An
Cleireach, 50. Bagh
Tharsgabhaig,
51. Bealach Udal,
52. Boirearaig-carn
Dearg, 53. Coille
Dalavil, 54. Coille
Thocabhaig, 55. Cuillins,

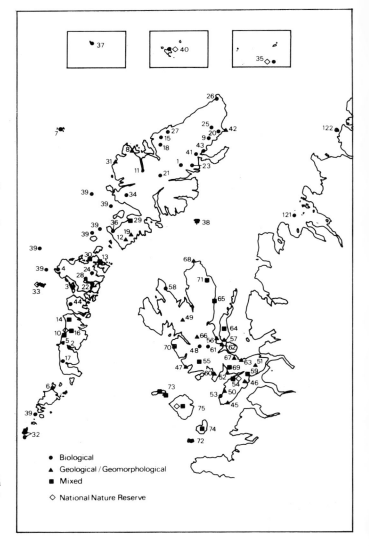

exploitation. The Hebrides are far from pristine, but they are comparatively unspoilt.

Maintaining and improving the natural diversity of the Hebrides is done by influencing man's use of land and sea through the selection and management of Sites of Special Scientific Interest (SSSIs). There is also statutory protection of species throughout the islands as a whole, as well as the provision of advice by Scottish Natural Heritage (SNH) and other conservation bodies.

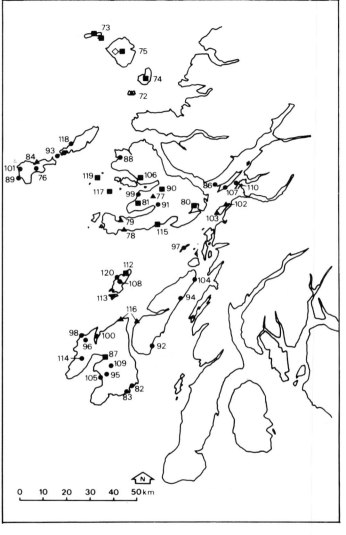

56. Druim Iosal, 57. Eyre
Point, 58. Geary Ravine,
59. Loch na Dal,
60. Loch Scavaig (Elgol
Coast), 61. Lochs at
Sligachan, 62. Meal a
Mhaoil, 63. Ob Lusa,
Ard Nis Coast,
64. Raasay, 65. Rigg-
Bile, 66. Roineval,
67. Rubh an
Eireannaich, 68. Rubha
Hunish, 69. Strath,
70. Talisker,
71. Trotternish Ridge
(Storr to Quirang),
72. Camus Mor, Muck,
73. Canna and Sanday,
74. Eigg, 75. Rum.
Figure 55b: southern
Inner Hebrides
76. An Fhaodhail and
The Reef, 77. An
Gearna, 78. Ardalanish
Bay, 79. Ardtun Leaf
Beds, 80. Ardura—
Auchnacraig,
81. Ardmeanach,
82. Ardmore and
Kildaton Woods,
83. Callumkill Wood,
84. Balepetrish,
85. Blank, 86. Bernera
Island, 87. Bridgend
Flats, 88. Calgary
Dunes, 89. Caenn a'
Mhara, 90. Central
Mull Complex,
91. Coladoir Bog,
92. Craighouse Ravine,
93. Crossapol and
Gunna, 94. Doire
Dhonn, 95. Eilean na
Muice Dubh, 96. Feur
Lochain,
97. Garvellachs,
98. Glac na Criche,
99. Gribun Shore and
Crags, 100. Gruinart
Flats, 101. Hough Bay
and Balevullin Machair,
102. Kerrera North,
103. Kerrera South,
104. Kinuachdrach,
105. Laggan Peninsula,
106. Laggan Ulva Wood,
107. Lismore Lochs,
108. Loch Fada,
109. Loch Tallant,
110. Lynn of Lorne
Isles, 111. Blank,
112. North Colonsay,
113. Oronsay,
114. Rhinns, 115. Ross
of Mull Coast,
116. South Ebudes
Raised Beaches,
117. Staffa,
118. Totamore Dunes,
119. Treshnish Isles,
120. West Colonsay
Seabird Cliffs, 121. Priest
Island (Eilean a'
Chleirich), 122. Handa

SSSIs are selected on two criteria: scientific, in terms of
geology (p. 85), geomorphology, botany, and zoology; and
philosophical, in terms of rarity, fragility, diversity, naturalness
and representativeness (Ratcliffe, 1977). The features of interest in earth science include rock types, crustal structures, landforms and erosion products, while in life science the features
are species or lifeforms, and habitats or ecosystems within
which the species live. Some species, for example the Arctic
sandwort, St Kilda mouse and wren, and the grey seal, can be

conserved within specific sites. Others, like the newts, golden eagle, corncrake, and pipistrelle bat, require some degree of protection wherever they occur.

SSSIs have existed since the National Parks and Access to the Countryside Act (Section 23) was placed on the *Statute Book* in 1949. However, it was not until the publication of *A Conservation Review* (NCR) (1977), that the SSSI series was put on a firm footing. The work was done by the Nature Conservancy Council (NCC) and the Natural Environment Research Council (NERC), which took some ten years to compile. It was edited by Dr Derek Ratcliffe, who wrote much of it, together with some thirty other authors, and twice that number of informants. Following the NCR, 'A Geological Conservation Review' was instituted by the NCC, and this is still in progress. While the NCR supports the biological SSSIs, the GCR does the same for the geological SSSIs and a Marine Nature Conservation Review is now also in progress.

The SSSI system in Great Britain has been reinforced by the Birds Directive (1979), and the Habitat Directive (1992) of the European Union. These directives are combined in the Natura 2000 Network (Scottish Natural Heritage, 1996). A number of the more valuable Hebridean SSSIs have been listed as Special Protection Areas (SPA) under the former, or Special Areas of Conservation (SAC) under the latter. In the following paragraphs describing the SSSIs in the Hebrides, all the sites mentioned by name are SSSIs (see Figs. 7 *a* and *b*).

Biological Sites

Coastal

The Hebrides abound in rocky and sandy shores of great beauty and interest; cliffs and beach platforms, tidal flats, estuaries, shelving shores and seabeds are arrayed against the prevailing conditions of exposure to, and shelter from, the weather and sea. The following are the most important coastal sites and habitats.

Rocky shores and seacliffs with seabirds, sea-sprayed grasslands, and ledge flora:—North Rona and Sula Sgeir, Flannan Islands, Shiant Islands, St Kilda, Mingulay and Berneray, Tiree (Ceann a'Mhara), Rum, Canna, Ardmeanach (Mull), Ross of Mull, Treshnish Isles.

Shell sand dunes and machair:—Luskentyre Banks, Northton Bay and Berneray (all Harris), Monach Islands, Robach and Newton, Baleshare and Kirkibost (all North Uist), Grogarry and Stilligarry, Bornish and Ormiclate (all South Uist),

Eoligarry (Barra), Balevullin and Barrapol (Tiree), Gunna and Totamore (Coll), Calgary (Mull) and Oronsay.

Other sand dunes and 'links':— Loch Gruinart, Laggan and Rhinns (all Islay), Kilmory (Rum); saltings and estuaries:— Loch Gruinart and Loch Indaal (Islay), Howmore (South Uist), Vallay and Loch an Duin (North Uist), Northton Bay (Harris) and Gress (Lewis).

Small island ecosystems, some having breeding seals:— Oronsay, Garvellachs, islets in the Lynn of Lorne, Treshnish Isles, Berneray, Mingulay, Pabbay, the Monach Isles, small seal islands (Haskeir, Shillay, Coppay, Gasker), St Kilda, the Shiant Islands, the Flannan Isles, North Rona and Sula Sgeir, Eilein a'Chleirich (Priest Island), and Handa.

Uplands

The massif of North Harris is representative of upland composed entirely of Lewisian gneiss, situated in the Atlantic storm-belt. These are among the most denuded hills in Britain, possessing a vegetation which, though poor in species, is rich in oceanic mosses. Rum has a wonderful variety of upland habitats, generated by the interaction of weather and an

A stag with hinds on Rum (Photo T. H. Clutton-Brock)

assortment of rocky substrates, and these are enhanced by the debris of mountain-top colonies of Manx shearwaters and the grazing of red deer, which help to create and maintain high altitude 'greens'. The Trotternish ridge in Skye has an extensive inland cliff-system with calcicolous flora and holds the finest montane flora in the Hebrides—plant communities which have affinities with the uplands of mainland Britain, Faeroes and Iceland. This site is also rich in upland birds. At a lower level, sub-montane, basaltic uplands of special interest are also present at Ardmeanach, Mull; Eigg and Canna.

Woodlands

Western oakwood persists in the Inner Hebrides, as fragments of a much more extensive aboriginal woodland. The interest of these woodlands is seen in a European context; the British Isles may hold many species of Atlantic bryophytes and lichens, and the Hebridean woods represent an extreme of biological variation in both Britain and Europe.

Coille Ardura, Mull is one of the largest fragments of the oak-ash-hazel community, and its character is reflected in the *Kinloch Wood SSSI* smaller remnants at Kinuachdrach, Jura. Smaller fragments *on the shores of Loch* still occur at a'Choille Mhor, Colonsay and at Ardmore-*na Dal, Skye (Photo* Claggain, Islay. There are other woods at Craighouse Ravine *J. M. Boyd)*

and Doire Dhonn, Jura; Craignure Cliffs and Laggan Wood, Mull and Coille Dalavil, Skye. Ashwood is scarce and is present only at Coille Ardura, Mull and Coille Thocabhaig and Loch na Dal, Skye (p. 90). There are no oak–ash–hazel stands in the Outer Hebrides, though such woodland may have grown there about 3,500 years ago.

In contrast, birch is widespread throughout the Hebrides, occurring often with oak in many of the above woods in the Inner Hebrides. Many small birch–rowan–willow woods have survived grazing and burning in stream gorges and in islands in freshwater lochs in both the Inner and Outer Hebrides. There are birch woods at Druimgigha (recently de-notified as an SSSI), Mull, the Geary Ravine and Allt Grillan, Skye. Far-western birchwoods also occur on the islands of Loch Druidibeg and at Allt Volagir, South Uist. Fine alderwoods are found at Ardmore, Kildalton and Calumhill, Islay; Kinuachdrach, Jura; and Loch na Dal, Skye. There are no stands of native pine in the Hebrides.

Inland Waters

The lochs are arranged in trophic (nutritional) order. Those with a rich status are termed *eutrophic*; intermediate, *mesotrophic*; poor, *oligotrophic*; very poor, *dystrophic*. However, because of the marine influence on the fresh waters of the Hebrides, resulting in higher than usual concentrations of some cations, many are anomalous in whatever trophic category they fall.

The alkaline machair lochs are generally mesotrophic and, more rarely, eutrophic in character, although they are not as biologically rich as one would normally expect for alkaline lochs, because generally they lack organic-based mud. They are represented in the Outer Hebrides by Lochs Stiapavat (Lewis), nam Feithean (North Uist), a'Mhachair, Stilligarry and Hallan (all South Uist); and in the Inner Hebrides by Lochs a' Phuill and Bhasapol (both in Tiree). Perhaps the only truly eutrophic loch in the Outer Hebrides is Loch a'Chinn Uacraich on Benbecula (R. N. B. Campbell, pers. comm.). Lochs situated on the ultrabasic rocks (very poor in calcium) of Rum, such as Loch Papadil, and on the limestones (very rich in calcium) of Raasay and Lismore (marl lochs) are especially interesting because of their unusual limnology.

The oligotrophic systems are situated between the shell sand machair and the acid peat moorland of which Lochs Bee and Roag-Fada (South Uist) are examples. All the other lochs on the list of SSSIs fall within the meso-oligotrophic range, situated in or fed directly from, moorland catchments. Lochs

Laxavat (Lewis), Scadavay (North Uist) and Druidibeg (South Uist), are good examples of the many acid lochs included in the series of SSSIs—some of these may be so acid as to be almost lifeless. Brackish water systems occur at Lochs Bee, Roag and Fada (South Uist) and Loch an Duin (North Uist).

Peatland and Bogs

Peatlands are widespread in the interiors of the islands. The large SSSIs—North Harris, Loch Druidibeg, Rum, Canna, Rhinns of Islay and Ardmeanach (Mull)—have many peatland habitats, and central and north Lewis have vast areas of blanket peat. In contrast to peatlands, bogs, which have not been drained or cut for fuel and still retain their natural form and communities, are uncommon. There are several types (see pp. 148–156, H-ANT) and some SSSIs hold more than one type merging into each other. On Lewis, the blanket bog at Achmore is 307ha. while the valley bogs at Loch Scarrasdale and Little Loch Roag are 207ha. and 19ha. respectively. On Skye, the valley bog at Loch an Eilein is 32ha. There is a raised bog at Coladoir on Mull, a blanket raised bog at Eilein na Muice Dubh (Duich Moss) on Islay (547ha.) and a watershed bog on Rhinns, Islay (8,403ha.)

Geological Sites

Lewisian, Torridonian, Moine

This is a major group of rock forms found on almost all the Outer Hebrides, Skye, Tiree, Coll, Iona, Colonsay, South Rona, the Summer Isles, Handa, Raasay, and Islay (Smith and Fettes, 1979; Bowes, 1983). At Loch na Dal, Sleat, the Kishorn Thrust separates the Lewisian gneiss and the Torridonian sandstone, and also in Sleat there is another classic section of the Moine strata by the Tarskavaig Thrust. At Balephetrish on Tiree, both ortho- and paragneisses, which have different origins, are exposed with veins of marble. At Ardlanish on Ross of Mull, the Moine schists exhibit progressive contact alterations as they approach the granite intrusion, and kyanite and tourmaline gneisses also occur on the site. On Colonsay, the Torridonian overlies unconformably the Lewisian, and the junction of the greywacke and arkose facies of the Torridonian is exposed. Kerrera has crumpled slates and limestones of Dalradian age overlain uncomformably by Lower Old Red Sandstone containing fossil fish. The sites in the Outer

Hebrides are at present under review but there are geological sites of special interest in the Lewisian complex at Tolsta Head, Glen Valtos, Loch Meurach, Loch a'Sgurr (pegmatite), Shiant Islands and Rockall.

Mesozoic

At Gribun on Mull, there is a key exposure for the student of Mesozoic palaeography. Moine schists are overlaid unconformably by Triassic sandstone and conglomerate with fine exposures of Triassic cornstone. In the bed of Allt nan Teangaidh, there is a series of strata from Triassic through Rhaetic to Cretaceous, with Upper Cretaceous Limestone resting unconformably on the Triassic rocks. This complements the nearby exposure of the Blue Lias lithologies at Aird na h'Iolaire. On the shore at Breakish in south-east Skye there is an exposure of the Lower Lias with the Lusa coral bed. Jurassic strata from Middle Lias to the base of the Great Estuarine Series are exposed at Rigg Holm Coast on Skye, and the sequence is continued at the Elgol coast below, which has exposures from the Great Estuarine Series to the Oxford Clays. Raasay has a compound site demonstrating the Mesozoic rocks of the Hebrides and a variety of Tertiary rocks with which they have been intruded. The youngest Jurassic rocks in the Hebrides are exposed on Mull, where shales of Kimeridge clay can be

Elgol coast geological SSSI, exposures of the Great Estuarine Series (Jurassic) on the shore of Loch Scavaig (Photo J. M. Boyd)

seen at Eas Mor, and the coast between Staffin and Kildorais holds classic sections of Oxford (rich in micro-fauna), Corellian and Lower Kimeridge Clays.

Tertiary

The Tertiary complexes of Rum, Skye, Canna, Mull and St Kilda are described in greater detail elsewhere in this book (see p. 38). Rum, Canna and St Kilda are geological SSSIs in their entirety. Along the coast of the Ross of Mull, the lava plateau overlies Tertiary sediments, including a wide range of lithologies, and rests on Cenomanian sandstone. A continuous section through the lower part of the plateau lavas is exposed at Ardmeanach, where lava tubes, flow units and scoria are seen, and pillow lavas occur at Glen Forsa, Mull. Ardmeanach also has fine displays of columnar jointing, which is a widespread characteristic of western Mull, Treshnish Islands, Canna and Sanday, north Skye and Heyskeir, and displayed *par excellence* on Staffa below. The volcanic centres of central Mull, Rum and cuillins of Skye and St Kilda are all represented in the series of geological SSSIs.

Staffa is an SSSI holding the world famous Tertiary rocks of Fingal's cave—columnar basalt par excellence *(Photo British Geological Survey)*

The Outer Hebrides are bereft of fossils, except, perhaps, in the Permian and Triassic sandstones on Lewis. The Inner Hebrides, however, have many sites of great interest in the Mesozoic and Tertiary rocks. Ardtun, Ross of Mull has 'leaf

beds', with lotus lily *Nelumbium* and *Magnolia*, suggesting a subtropical climate in Tertiary times prior to and during the volcanic activity. Other beds contain fossils of the maidenhair tree *Ginkgo*, plane tree *Platanus*, hazel and oak. There are few examples in Europe of this Tertiary flora and Mull possesses the only fossil plants of Miocene and Pliocene age in Britain. MacCulloch's tree at Ardmeanach is thought to be of Eocene age (*c*. 60 million years). On Skye there are several fossil-rich sites including Rigg-Holm coast, Boreraig-Carn Dearg, and Staffin-Kildorais coast (Trotternish SSSI), and there is a key vertebrate fossil site of mid-late Bethonian age at Loch Scavaig.

Marine Conservation

There are no SSSIs below low water mark; no such measures have been taken for nature conservation in the sea and the seabed. However, under Sections 26 and 37 of the Wildlife and Countryside Act, the Secretary of State for Scotland can desig-nate marine nature reserves up to the seaward limits of terri-torial waters. No such reserves have yet been created in Scotland, but the SNH has identified Marine Consultation Areas of which nine fall within the Hebrides (Fig. 8). Conser-vation of the marine environment lags far behind what has been achieved on land, and efforts are now being made to obtain a more satisfactory form of marine nature conservation.

The technical advances in Scuba diving in the last 30 years have made possible the exploration of the shallow coastal seas. There is now a thriving Marine Conservation Society and a growing cadre of scientists, who are at once expert in this tech-nique and also in a specialist field of marine survey. The paral-lel growth of knowledge of marine species and sub-littoral habitats, which hitherto were almost closed to the observer, are now readily accessible to the Scuba diver. However, under-water surveys are far more demanding on manpower than those on land, and progress is slow by comparison. The remoteness and tempestuous nature of the Hebrides adds to the difficulties of diving surveys (Mitchell *et al.* 1983).

The Hebrides have a great variety of shore, seabed and water-column habitats influenced by tidal currents, freshwater run-off, and exposure to surf, and the whole realm needs classification and evaluation in scientific and philosophical terms. The Marine Nature Conservation Review is now in progress and will last ten years. In it the biota are divided into communities on rock and sediment, and each of these is subdivided into categories of exposure to surf, and of specialised niches e.g. crevices, tidal rips, and man-made

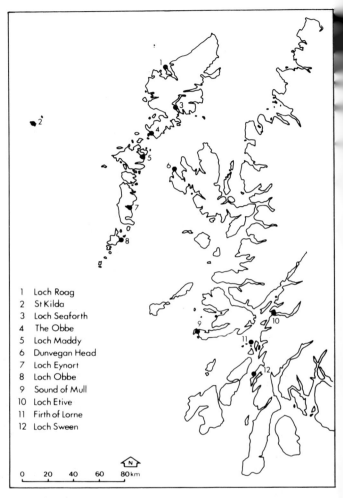

1 Loch Roag
2 St Kilda
3 Loch Seaforth
4 The Obbe
5 Loch Maddy
6 Dunvegan Head
7 Loch Eynort
8 Loch Obbe
9 Sound of Mull
10 Loch Etive
11 Firth of Lorne
12 Loch Sween

0   20   40   60   80km

Fig. 8
*Map showing the
distribution of Marine
Conservation Areas in
the Hebrides (from
Nature Conservancy
Council)*

structures. Future editions of this book should carry much
more information in these current endeavours in marine
nature conservation.

Nature Reserves

At present, there are seventeen reserves in the Western
Isles of Scotland: six National Nature Reserves (NNR)
managed by the SNH, four by the RSPB, five as island
properties of the National Trust for Scotland (NTS), one
by the Scottish Wildlife Trust (SWT) and one which has
been recently acquired by the Woodland Trust (Fig. 9).

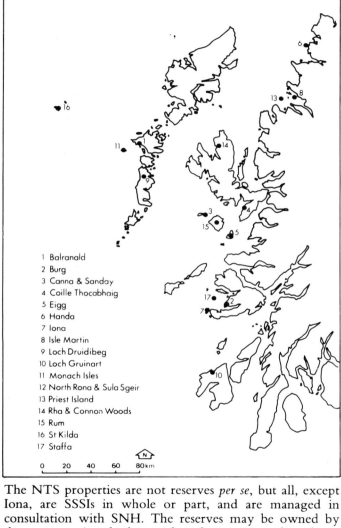

1 Balranald
2 Burg
3 Canna & Sanday
4 Coille Thocabhaig
5 Eigg
6 Handa
7 Iona
8 Isle Martin
9 Loch Druidibeg
10 Loch Gruinart
11 Monach Isles
12 North Rona & Sula Sgeir
13 Priest Island
14 Rha & Connon Woods
15 Rum
16 St Kilda
17 Staffa

0 20 40 60 80km

Fig. 9
Map showing the distribution of Nature Reserves in the Hebrides

The NTS properties are not reserves *per se*, but all, except Iona, are SSSIs in whole or part, and are managed in consultation with SNH. The reserves may be owned by the conservation body, or leased or managed under a formal agreement with the owner. For example, St Kilda is owned by the NTS, and leased as a nature reserve by the SNH. 'Privatisation' of the NNRs would only affect Rum and part of Loch Druidibeg which are areas owned by the government-sponsored SNH.

Balranald

The reserve (658ha.) in North Uist is an SSSI with machair, lagoon (Loch nam Feithean), swamp and fringing marshes. It has a high density of breeding waders, wildfowl and corn-crakes, and is privately owned croftland with the wildlife managed by the RSPB in agreement with owners and tenant crofters.

Burg

The area (617ha.) in Mull has been owned by the NTS since 1932. Called 'The Widerness', it was the first nature reserve in the Hebrides owned by a conservation body. It is situated at the western tip of the Ardmeanach peninsula, and has a spectacular rocky coastline of columnar basalt, in which is embedded 'MacCulloch's Tree' (see p. 95). It has fine marine and coastal communities, possessing relict woodland, calcicolous grassland with abundant lepidoptera, and good acidic grassland and montane flora. The whole property lies within the Ardmeanach SSSI.

Canna and Sanday

These islands were owned and managed for fifty years by Dr J. L. Campbell as a private nature reserve in the context of an island estate. Since 1981, they have been a Property of the NTS. There are fine marine, coastal, and upland habitats, colonies of seabirds and well-grown mixed woodland. These islands are a complex of columnar-basalt landforms. Both islands (except the enclosed agricultural land) are an SSSI (1,469ha.)

Coille Thocabhaig

This reserve (81ha.) in Skye, known also as Ord Wood, lies on neighbouring outcrops of the Durness limestone and Torridonian sandstone. There is ash on the limestone and oak on the sandstone, and the reserve has been established to maintain the varied broadleaved woodland of native species, and the several distinct associations of plants in the ash and oak habitats. It is one of the richest localities in Scotland for 'oceanic' mosses. Though it is sheep pasture, three grazing enclosures of 10ha. have been made so far (two on limestone and one on sandstone) to assist in regenerating the woodland. This is an SSSI which has recently ceased to be an NNR.

Eigg

Three areas (total 1,517ha.) of Eigg are a nature reserve: one area includes the Sgurr with surrounding upland and wetland habitats; a second is situated in the interior of the island and is dominated by willow/birch/hawthorn woodland; a third is the area below the cliffs of Beinn Bhuide, running the length of the east coast of the island, round the north point, and below the west-facing cliffs of Cleadale. This last contains a colony of Manx shearwaters and gallery woodlands of hazel, elm and oak on basalt screes. All areas are part of the complex of SSSIs on Eigg and they are managed by the SWT under an agreement with the owner and tenant crofters.

Handa

The reserve (310ha.) has large colonies of seabirds arrayed in horizontally bedded Torridonian sandstone in perpendicular cliffs, providing ideal nesting habitat for kittiwakes, guillemots and razorbills. It is managed by the SWT under an agreement with the owner, and is an SSSI.

Iona

Most of the island is a property of the NTS and is enclosed cultivated land with machair and maritime heath on Torridonian/Lewisian rocks with veins of marble. It is not a nature reserve or an SSSI, but is a fine specimen of the small fertile Hebridean isle, complete with its historical abbey and burial grounds, which attract thousands of visitors annually.

Isle Martin

This reserve (52ha.) is situated at the mouth of Loch Broom and is owned by the RSPB. It is a typical assemblage of coastal and acid grassland and heathland habitats, situated on the Torridonian rocks of the north-west Highlands. The island is set in the wild scenery of Coigach.

Loch Druidibeg

The reserve (1,677ha.) is an SSSI situated in the crofting townships of Grogarry, Stilligarry and Howmore on South Uist (see Chapter 10). It is of international importance, recognised under the Ramsar Convention on Wetlands, for its open freshwater system which has a wide range of trophic levels with related communities of plants and animals, including the native greylag goose. It is of national importance for its coastal habitats including lagoon, dune and machair. The reserve also contains peatland, cultivated croftland and scrub woodland on islands in the Loch. It is partly owned by the SNH and the remainder is managed under agreement with the owners and crofters.

Loch Gruinart

The reserve (1,554ha.) lies to the south and west of Loch Gruinart in Islay. There are two main habitats—grassland on Gruinart Flats, and moorland. There are also important saltings, marshes, lochans and small woods. The reserve is owned by the RSPB, who manage the land for wild geese with the use of a suckler herd of 260 cattle and the reseeding of the grasslands. In the season 1987–88, at least 7,000 barnacle geese (one third of the population of Islay) used the reserve from October to March, and in October-November some 17,000 used the reserve for feeding and roosting. There are also many other

species of wildfowl, waders, raptors and songbirds that regularly use the reserve. The reserve includes part of a large SSSI, and its aims in the conservation of wild geese are augmented by agreements between the SNH and local tenant farmers, whose ground falls within the SSSI. These agreements stipulate that the tenants will forgo their rights as agricultural occupiers to protect their crops, including rotational leys, permanent pasture and rough grazings, from damage from barnacle and white-fronted geese, and in return receive compensation on the net profit foregone (p. 52).

The RSPB Reserve at Loch Gruinart, Islay (Photo Morley Hedley)

Monach Isles

These are five uninhabited islands in North Uist: Ceann Ear (193ha.), Ceann Iar (135ha.), Shivinish (28ha.), Shillay (16ha.), and Stockay (3ha.). The reserve (375ha.) is an SSSI, which includes systems of shell-sand dunes and machair with a rich flora and the most western oceanic fresh water lochs in Britain. In autumn these islands are the largest nursery colony of the grey seal in Britain, with over 2,500 pups born annually. In winter they are a refuge for about 2,000 barnacle geese, and in summer they have many nesting species of birds. Most of the Monach Isles are owned privately and Shillay is owned by the Northern Lighthouse Board. The wildlife is managed by the SNH under agreement (see Chapter 5, H-AMI).

North Rona and Sula Sgeir

These are two uninhabited islands. The reserve (130ha.) is an SSSI and holds oceanic vegetation and important breeding assemblies of seabirds and grey seals. It is privately owned and the wildlife is managed by the SNH by agreement with the owners. Both islands now have automatic lighthouses.

Priest Island

This reserve (121ha.) is also known as Eilean a' Chleirich, and is the outermost of the Summer Isles. It is an uninhabited trenched platform of Torridonian sandstone with a rocky exposed coast, a number of small lochans, a tidal lagoon, heathery ridges and hillocks and wet, sedgy hollows. Breeding colonies of seabirds attracted Frank Fraser Darling to the island for his studies of gull flocks in 1936–37. The reserve is owned by the RSPB and is an SSSI.

Rha and Conon Woods

Two gorge woods at Uig in Skye which have been acquired as a reserve by the Woodland Trust. The gorges are very steep-sided, may have contained woods since before man came to the Hebrides, and have a history of ancient woodland. Today they hold a community of rowan, alder, hawthorn, sycamore and hazel with a diverse ground flora, on Tertiary lavas and Jurassic sediment, in country which is generally lacking in trees.

Rum

We have devoted Chapter 15 to Rum; here we provide some basic facts only. The island (10,684ha.) is an SSSI and is owned by the Nature Conservancy Council. It is a National Nature Reserve under section 19 of the National Parks and Access to the Countryside Act, 1949. Rum has also been designated as a Biosphere Reserve (BR), under the Man and Biosphere Programme of UNESCO. The main features are the wide range of rocks, soils and vegetation; the large breeding colonies of Manx shearwaters; an insular population of red deer; an array of sylvicultural experiments in the exposed environment of the

Hebrides; a succinct island ecosystem of which the inventory of plants and animals is highly advanced. Rum is a research reserve into which visitors can venture within the management regime of the SNH. Over the last thirty years, public funds have been invested in Rum because of its part in conserving the national heritage in wildlife. The island is a world-class nature reserve in which management should continue in the hands of the SNH or a national conservation body of equivalent status; a private owner could not be expected to fulfil the purposes for which the reserve was created.

St Kilda

There are four islands: Hirta (638ha., 426m), Soay (99ha., 373m), Boreray (77ha., 380m), and Dun (32ha.; 175m). There are many sea-stacks of which Stac an Armin (190m) and Stac Lee (172m) are the largest. We have described the reserve (853ha.) in Chapter 16. It is an SSSI of international importance for its oceanic vegetation, assemblies of breeding seabirds, indigenous fauna of the St Kilda field mouse, the St Kilda wren, and Soay sheep. Part of the value of the reserve is in the opportunities it presents for scientific studies of its wildlife. It also has a well studied history of occupation by man and a considerable literature. St Kilda is owned by the NTS and is managed as a nature reserve by the SNH. At present Hirta has a military garrison which operates within agreed limits. The tripartite operation of the islands between the NTS (owners), SNH (lessees) and the Army (sub-leasees) has been very successful. Indeed, St Kilda was the first natural area in UK to be accepted by UNESCO under the World Heritage Convention in 1987.

Staffa

The island (45ha.) was made world famous by Felix Mendelssohn and his overture *The Hebrides* or *Fingal's Cave* composed in 1830, which has a fixed place in the repertoire of popular classical music, so evocative is it of the sea, the islands, and the great echoing vault of Fingal's Cave cutting deep into the island. The geological structures in columnar basalt are exquisite; Fingal's Cave is like a cathedral. The island is owned by the NTS and it is an SSSI on both geological and biological grounds (p. 94).

Protected Species

The conservation of habitat in SSSIs and nature reserves contributes much to the conservation of all species and communities in the Hebrides. Some SSSIs have been created to conserve certain species, for example, the gannet at St Kilda and Sula Sgeir and the grey seal at the Monach Isles, Gasker and North Rona. However, other species which are widespread in distribution, and uncertain in annual location, cannot be easily managed by site conservation; for example, divers, eagles and other raptors, corncrakes, otters, bats and newts. Such species require the added protection of the law wherever they occur.

Table 20.1 shows those species in the Hebrides which have this statutory safeguard under the Wildlife and Countryside Act 1981. This list will change in time, on the one hand by statutory amendment, on the other by the discovery in the Hebrides of protected species not previously recorded. For example, the wood sandpiper (*Tringa glareola*), fieldfare (*Turdus pilaris*), redwing (*Turdus iliaca*), Daubenton's bat (*Myotis daubentoni*) and the arctic-alpine plant (*Diapensia lapponica*) may soon be found to reproduce in the Hebrides. The complete list of protected species in Great Britain is given in the above Act (HMSO, 1981). Red deer and roe deer are covered by The Deer Act 1963, grey seals and common seals by The Conservation of Seals Act 1970, and badgers (unrecorded from the Hebrides, so far) by The Badgers Act 1973.

Schedule 1—Birds which breed in the Hebrides, and which are protected by special penalties.

English	Scientific	Gaelic
A. At all times		
Red-throated diver	*Gavia stellata*	*Learga-chaol*
Black-throated diver	*Gavia arctica*	*Learga-dhubh*
Leach's petrel	*Oceanodroma leucorhoa*	*Gobhlan-mara*
Whooper swan	*Cygnus cygnus*	*Eala-fhiadhaich*
Scaup	*Aythya marila*	*Lach-mhara*
Common scoter	*Melanitta nigra*	*Lach-bheag-dhubh*
White-tailed eagle	*Haliaetus albicilla*	*Iolaire-mhara*
Hen harrier	*Circus cyaneus*	*Clamhan-nan-cearc*
Golden eagle	*Aquila chrysaetos*	*Iolaire-bhuidhe*
Merlin	*Falco columbarius*	*Meirneal*
Peregrine	*Falco peregrinus*	*Seabhag*
Corncrake	*Crex crex*	*Traona*
Black-tailed godwit	*Limosa limosa*	*Cearra-ghob*
Greenshank	*Tringa nebularia*	*Deoch-bhiugh*
Whimbrel	*Numenius phaeopus*	*Eun-bealltainn*

English	Scientific	Gaelic
Red-necked phalarope	*Phalaropus lobatus*	*Deargan*
Roseate tern	*Sterna dougallii*	*Stearnal-Dhughaill*
Little tern	*S. albifrons*	*Stearnal-beag*
Barn owl	*Tyto alba*	*Comhachag*
Chough	*Pyrrhocorax pyrrhocorax*	*Cathag-dhearg-chasach*
B. During the Close Season		
Greylag goose	*Anser anser+*	*Geadh-glas*
Pintail	*Anas acuta*	*Lach-stiuireach*

+Outer Hebrides only

Schedule 5—Animals in the Hebrides, which are protected against killing, injury, taking possession of or sale.

Common toad	*Bufo bufo**	*Muile-mhag*
Common frog	*Rana temporaria**	*Losgann*
Palmate newt	*Triturus helveticus**	⎫ *Dearc-luachrach*
Smooth newt	*T. vulgaris**	⎭
Viviparous lizard	*Lacerta vivipara*	
Slow worm	*Anguis fragilis**	*Nathair-challtainn*
Adder	*Vipera berus**	*Nathair-nimhe*
Whales/dolphins/porpoises:	All species	
Walrus	*Odobenus rosmarus*	
Otter	*Lutra lutra*	*Dobhran*
Pipistrelle bat	*Pipistrellus pipistrellus*	*Ialtag-phipistrelle*
Long-eared bat	*Plecotus auritus*	*Ialtag-chluasach*
Turtles	All species	

*Against sale or possession without intent to sell only.

Schedule 8—Plants of the Hebrides which are protected

Alpine catchfly	*Lychnis alpina*
Alpine rockcress	*Arabis alpina*
Arctic sandwort	*Arenaria norvegica*
Purple coltsfoot	*Homogyne alpina*
Greater yellow-rattle	*Rhinanthus serotinus*

Table 6   Birds, animals and plants in the Hebrides which are protected under the Wildlife & Countryside Act, 1981.

CHAPTER 7

Epilogue—a Habitable Land?

Dr Samuel Johnson, in his Journey to the Western Islands of Scotland (1773), made Georgian Britain aware of the Hebrides as no previous author had done. Though Johnson's account was altogether forbidding to his contemporaries in England, it told also of a people whose gentleness, elegance, beauty, and gaiety contrasted with the savagery of their native land. Johnston spoke of the gentry by whom he was lodged and entertained, but a century later Lord Napier spoke of the ordinary people. The crofters and cottars in their sordid hovels, he reported to Parliament, did not show physical and moral degradation, but decency, courtesy, virtue and mental refinement. How could such poverty of worldly possessions generate such a richness of soul?

The Hebrideans are not unique in this respect, for recently in our travels we have found the same dignity of life in the face of deprivation among island peoples in Oceania. The ancestral movement of maritime people by great feats of seamanship and navigation in frail craft, from distant continental origins to the primeval islands, have set them apart from the rest of the world. Each became a race unto itself which, in the course of history, has received strangers from other origins, and become mixed both in kind and culture. The process continues today as a worldwide issue in which the insular aboriginals of the oceanic archipelagos are being displaced by immigrant continentals. In this the Hebrides are not immune; they are part of a world movement of peoples.

Strung out on the Atlantic edge of Europe, a stone's throw from the mainland, the Hebrides do not have the oceanic credentials of the New Hebrides. It was James Cook who gave these Pacific islands their name, because of their similar profile to the Western Isles of Scotland, and today there is another uncanny comparison. The survival of the Gaels and their culture which has, in history, absorbed the incursion of the Norsemen, now faces the settlement of large numbers of ethnic mainlanders. In the New Hebrides, now the Republic of

Vanuatu, the aboriginal Melanesians—Indo-Malay people—have, in their history, endured the incursion of the Polynesians, and now face the widespread infiltration of ethnic Chinese. 'Old' and 'New' Hebrideans have similar histories and face similar problems in the safeguard of their heritages, and their natural resources.

The once peaceful and fruitful islands have become progressively stripped of their natural resources, polluted and eroded. From a primitive age of pristine plenty when there was enough for all and more, there has come a modern age of natural poverty and human want. The 'want not' culture of the developed world of which the Hebrides is a part, contrasts with the 'want' culture of the New Hebrides. In the islands of Indonesia and Melanesia

Croft corn on 'lazy beds' harvested by scything and gathering by hand in Scarp, Harris, October 1953 (Photo: J. M. Boyd)

there is a burgeoning populace, tribal feudalism and no agricultural or social state subsidies. The tropical volcanic islands, unlike the temperate or granitic islands, remain productive · even under severe human population pressures. Both have lost, or are rapidly losing, their forests, but while the Hebrides become bog-ridden, the hills and valleys of the tropical islands are transformed by rice culture—the most intricate patterns of terraced paddies clothe hill and valley. Fraser Darling, who saw so much wrong with the way mankind had treated the Highlands and Islands of Scotland, was heard to exclaim on looking out on an Asian valley of terraced rice: 'Now here we see man's wooing of the land!'

The imperative of self-sufficiency which shaped the life of the Hebrideans before the advent of the welfare state in Britain, and which still prevails to a great extent in the Third World, has all but disappeared. The great spreads of *feannagan*, or 'lazy beds', in both the Outer and Inner Hebrides are a lasting testimony to the enormous physical effort required to make the islands productive of the basic needs of survival and habitability. It is the tragedy of Hebridean history that the islands proved less than habitable for many of their people. The Clearances of the 18th and 19th centuries had their atrocities, which resulted in too many people on too little fertile land, malnutrition, disease, starvation and death. Had the land been more equitably shared among the people, the disaster would have been less severe, but the potato blight would still have taken its toll.

The increase in the Hebridean population in the 18th and early 19th centuries was stimulated by the kelp industry. The Napoleonic War cut off Spanish supplies of barilla, an impure form of sodium carbonate used in making of soda products, and present in the ash of burned seaweed. The coastal clan chiefs found themselves in clover with the lucrative production of kelp, or whole ash of seaweed, from the shores of their estates. The industry was labour-intensive, and the labour force came from the tenantry. Rents were paid in hours worked, and work in excess of rent was paid in meal. This resulted in an increase in number and size of cottar families, and in the growing need for food.

The crofting system was installed by landowners in the 1820s to raise the efficiency of agriculture and increase food production. Waterloo not only brought down Napoleon; it restored the supply of Spanish barilla and brought down the kelp industry. Many landowners, who

had expended the profits of kelp, faced bankruptcy, and the cottars faced starvation. The population maximum occurred about 1840, and the potato famine of 1846–50 was a tragedy which was waiting to happen. Since then the populations of the islands have been in decline, with many of the outliers becoming uninhabited—the deserted villages on North Rona, Scarp, Monach, Mingulay, and St Kilda (now occupied by the Army) are poignant milestones in this melancholy history.

The ruins of crofting township on the Monach Islands overblown with shell sand and carpetted with machair (Photo: J. M. Boyd)

The population flux which resulted from the potato famine showed that the islands had become habitable by large numbers of people only because of the introduction of the potato. The potato was a subsidy in kind which, when suddenly withdrawn, caused devastation. There is no direct comparison with the present day, but if the cash support systems for agriculture, fisheries, and fish farming were to be reduced or withdrawn, shades of the Clearances and potato famine would follow in the Highlands and Islands. The recent disappearance of cereal and root crops from crofting land in favour of grazing, the reversion to rush and sedge on recently reclaimed hill pastures, and the reduction in animal husbandry through the effects of the Common Agricultural Policy of the EU all point to a dispiriting decline in agriculture which the subsidy system seems unable to reverse. It affects small-holdings on the entire western seaboard of the British Isles from Dingle to Unst, and is severe in the Hebrides. It is a paradox that, while the land is in dereliction, the homesteads (many as 'second homes' or the homes of

Prawn, scallop, crab and lobster boats crammed within the tiny fishing harbour at Kallin in Grimsay, North Uist (Photo: J. M. Boyd)

incomers) are in fine repair partly through a different, unconnected system of subsidies. Any suggestion of withdrawal of subsidy or services from NW Scotland brings a spontaneous cry of 'second clearances' from island communities, unmindful of the unmitigated clearance of the British countryside since the installation of the enclosures in the 18th and early 19th centuries, and of the drastic die-back of urban centres in more recent times. Deprivation and poverty extends far beyond the limits of the Hebrides, but the continuing decline of the agricultural industry is making these islands progressively uninhabitable by farmers who have been the staple of the island communities for 6,000 years.

Much of what is said of agriculture can be said of fisheries. At a time when the term 'sustainability' is being espoused by Government and people, in advance of a clear definition of its meaning and application in human affairs, the fishery of the Hebridean shelf is an object lesson in 'unsustainability'. The lack of any notion of conservation of fish stocks, either through instinct or by careful calculation and regulation by fishermen, has seen the virtual destruction of the other great staple of community life in the islands, the fishing industry. Over succeeding generations, the unsupervised fisherman, confronted with riches, simply took home as much as he could carry, in a century-long bonanza. The greed and glut of the grandfather and father has become the impoverishment of the son and grandson. The island fleets have disappeared, but the klondyking and juggernauting of huge quantities of fish and shell-fish out of Hebridean waters still goes on. The damage has long since been done, the pillar has fallen, and what remains is only of consequence as an employment to a much reduced number of fishermen mostly from the mainland, and as a blighted seed stock of fish for a future age. On the bright side, the decline in agriculture, fishing and the cottage weaving industry has been accompanied by the growth of fish farming and tourism, both of which are modern industries subject to the market forces in mainland Britain and Europe.

The Hebrides have a great appeal to people who live in mainland Britain and continental Europe. The scenery, wildlife, history, Gaelic culture and the customs and hospitality of the people are the main attractions cited in the tourist brochures. To the specialist visitor there is sailing, angling, wind surfing, hiking and biking, climbing and an abundance of wildlife, particularly birds and flowers. There is no lack of incentive, so why are the islands not overrun by visitors? There is not a simple answer, but the greatest disincentive is the weather. The Atlantic storm-belt even in July can produce 10 cms of rain, one sunny day in three, one calm day in five, average temperatures of about 15°C, and a relative humidity of about 85 per cent. The combination of high humidity and high wind speed off-sets the advantages of a high sunshine quota, and has an adverse effect on human comfort, particularly of the visitor who is unprepared for runs of wet and windy days. When the weather is calm and warm the Hebrides are idyllic, but some are also famous for their midges, the bane of unprepared campers and walkers in the Inner Hebrides from June to September.

A backward look to mediaeval life in the islands, with a wet, stormy climate similar to that of today, and a reliance on the six-eared oat in the absence of the potato, shows that winter hardship, suffering and want was followed by summer ease, gaiety, and sufficiency. Upon this seasonal rhythm of privation and prosperity, there was borne the agony and ecstasy of the people, the elemental stuff of their being from which sprang the inspiration of music, song, poetry and dance. The break point came when this delicate rhythm of life was shattered by the Clearances and the agony of the potato famine beyond which there was no ecstasy, only a longing for the return of a bygone golden time of peace and plenty, of heroes and champions, of virtue and sweet contentment. But was this longing for a golden time a myth created by the Victorians both at home and in the Empire, out of sentiment for an epic tragedy?

*The British European
Airways service from
Glasgow via Tiree (De
Havilland 'Heron')
landed on the Cockls
Strand, Barra in 1970
(Photo: J. M. Boyd*

. . .

> Yet still the blood is strong, the heart is Highland,
> And we in dreams behold the Hebrides.

The Hebrideans do not have a written saga like the
Orcadians, but within the misery of starvation, death and
disruption of family life, they possess a nostalgia for the
legendary Tir nan Og—the Land of the Ever Young.
This nostalgia went with them to their emigrant homesteads in America and Australia and the mushrooming
tenements of Clydeside, and became the evocation of
Gaelic verse and song.

. . .

Bheir mi ò ro bhan ò	Vair me oro van o,
Bheir mi ò ro bhan i	Vair me ore van ee.
Bheir mi ò ru ò hò	Vair me oro o ho,
'S mi tha brònach 's tu 'm dhìth	Sad I am without thee.

Sadly, the historians of the Gaelic people in search of a
bygone golden age cannot find it in the Hebrides.
Perhaps there remains deeper recall of Eldorado from
prehistory; of times more distant in the stages of their
great journey through the millenia to these islands, from
the Caspian Sea, through Mediterranean lands, Iberia and
Hibernia. The palaeoecology points to the settlement by
the Celtic people in a Hebridean environment, hostile by
comparison with those in the south from whence they
came. In the earliest times of the Mesolithic, the first
hunter/fisher/gatherers, though living gregariously, would
be few and far between. They had rich resources in food,
fuel and shelter in an ameliorating climate which was
sustained throughout the arrival and settlement of the
early Neolithic farmers of the fourth millenium BC. On
the basic ecological essentials of life at a human climatic
optimum, the golden age might have occurred at a point

deep in pre-history. The well-spaced early farming communities and their livestock had not yet stripped the islands of their trees, gashed the light sandy loams with their ploughs, or scorched the hill pastures by burning the dead forage. In the Atlantic and Sub-boreal periods—1000 to 4000 BC—the climate was warmer and, on the whole, probably drier and less windy than it is today. The islands would be well forested, replete with maritime soils, and would have an abundance of wildlife. The seas, shores, rivers and lochs would be prolific in diverse whales, seals, fish and fowl. Subject to there being no widespread endemic ill-health, or internecine strife, and to the modest demands of a peasant life-style, we have a recipe for a time of sustained self-sufficiency, unaffected by the outside world—the golden time of the Hebridean psyche. Nothing since could have been its equal for tranquillity and happiness. Does it beggar belief that such a time of self-sufficiency might yet return to these islands? Does the plough lie rusting in the nettles, and the net lie rotting in the tangle—for ever?

The romance of the Hebrides has its origins partly in prehistory and partly in mythology. Was the assignment of Atlas to carry the sky upon his shoulders, and the guarding of the golden apples by his daughters, the Hesperides, in gardens set on the western edge of the known world, not laid by the Greeks in the path of the migratory Celtic people? 'The Golden Age of Gaeldom' envisaged by the Victorians may indeed have its roots in ancient oral tradition brought forward over millenia in legend and lore, but it is myth and not reality. The Atlantic storm-belt climate, the unyielding rock of the outer islands, the worn-out condition of soils and pasture and the impoverished marine and freshwater fisheries are the ecological realities of the modern Hebrides. Yet the romanticism of a habitable prosperous land still persists in the absence of any semblance of the self-sufficiency which has been the hallmark of island life since time immemorial.

It is a paradox that the very factors which make the islands forbidding and uninhabitable hold the keys to their future prosperity and settlement. The energies of the winds, seas and possibly also in the sunshine of the Atlantic storm belt are vast and, so far, have not been harvested on a commercial scale. The Outer Hebrides must be one of the most favoured platforms in Europe for the harvesting of 'clean' renewable power, and such a development on a commercial scale could transform life in

One-time cottar homes among the sand dunes at the The Green, Kilmaluag, Tiree now, holiday/retirement homes preserved in vernacular form complete with tarred roofs (Photo: J. M. Boyd)

north-west Scotland. Is it too imaginative to see a new island culture based on these almost unlimited resources of natural power, and on the electronic networks which shrink time and distance, and not only provide communication, but banish the isolation and loneliness which demoralise and ultimately extinguish island communities? If these technologies can be dove-tailed with a renaissance of ancestral values of self-reliance and self-sufficiency in work and leisure, there comes the vision of the ideal habitable land—a land epitomised by the bliss of Wordsworth on seeing a young woman cutting corn in a remote Highland glen.

> Behold her, single in the field,
> Yon solitary Highland Lass!
> Reaping and singing by herself;
> Stop here, or gently pass!
> . . .
> No nightingale did ever chant
> More welcome notes to weary bands
> Of travellers in some shady haunt,
> Among Arabian sands:
> A voice so thrilling ne'er was heard
> In spring-time from the cuckoo-bird,
> Breaking the silence of the seas
> Among the farthest Hebrides.

The Hebrides are no longer remote. They can be reached by aircraft in an hour or so, where it took weeks for Dr Samuel Johnson in 1773, and days for Hugh Miller in 1844 on the same journey. Yet despite the great changes of today, the advances of technology, and social and political restructuring, the Hebrides are still on 'the edge of the world'!

Bibliography

Atkinson, R. (1949). *Island Going*. Birlinn, Edinburgh.

Atkinson, R. (1980). *Shillay and the Seals*. Collins Harvill, London.

Bailey, R. S., Hislop, J. R. G. & Mason, J. (1979). The fish and shelfish resources in seas adjacent to the Outer Hebrides. *Proc. Roy. Soc. Edinb.* 77B, 479–494.

Balfour, E. J. (1979). Plants and people. In *Wildlife of Scotland* ed. F. Holliday, pp. 173–186.

Balfour, J. H. (1844). Account of a botanical excursion to Skye and the Outer Hebrides during the month of August 1841 and a catalogue of the plants gathered in the islands of North Uist, Harris and Lewis, during the month of August 1841. *Trans. Bot. Soc. Edinb.* 1, 133–154.

Balfour-Brown, F. (1953). The aquatic coleoptera of the Western Scottish Islands with a discussion of their sources of origin and means of arrival. *Entomologist's Gaz.* 23, 1–71.

Bannerman, J. (1986). *The Beatons: a medical kindred in the classical Gaelic tradition.* John Donald, Edinburgh.

Bennett, A. (1905). Supplement to *Topographic Botany* 2nd ed. *J. Bot. Lond.* 48, Suppl.

Bennett, A., Salmon, C. E. & Matthews, J. R. (1929–30). 2nd Supplement to *Topographic Botany* 2nd ed. *J. Bot. Lond.* 62 & 63, Suppl.

Berry, R. J. (1979). The Outer Hebrides: where genes and geography meet. *Proc. Roy. Soc. Edinb.* 77B, 21–43.

Berry, R. J. (1983). Evolution of animals and plants in the Inner Hebrides. *Proc. Roy. Soc. Edinb.* 83B, 433–447.

Bishop, G. M. (1987). The impact of an expansion of the Scottish fin fish aquaculture industry on wild fish stocks used to supply fishmeal components of feedstuffs. Unpubl. report of the World Wildlife Fund (UK), 14 pp, Godalming, Surrey.

Boswell, J. (1924). *Journal of a tour to the Hebrides with Samuel Johnson, LLD.* (1773). Oxford University Press.

Boyd, A. (1986). *Seann Taighean Tirisdeach.* Cairdean nan Tiaghean Tugha.

Boyd, J. M. (1957). The ecological distribution of the Lumbricidae in the Hebrides. *Proc. Zool. Soc. Lond.* 66B, 311–338.

Boyd, J. M. (1960b). Studies of the differences between fauna of grazed and ungrazed grassland in Tiree, Argyll, *Proc. Zool. Soc. Lond.* 135, 33–54.

Boyd, J. M. (ed.) (1979). The Natural Environment of the Outer Hebrides. *Proc. Roy. Soc. Edinb.* 77B, 561pp.

Boyd, J. M. (1983a). Natural Environment of the Inner Hebrides: an introduction. *Proc. Roy. Soc. Edinb.* 83B, 3–22.

Boyd, J. M. (1983b). Two hundred years of biological sciences in Scotland. Nature Conservation. *Proc. Roy. Soc. Edinb.* 84B, 295–336.

Boyd, J. M. (1986). *Fraser Darling's Islands.* Edinburgh University Press, Edinburgh.

Boyd, J. M. & Bowes, D. R. (eds.) (1983). The Natural Environment of the Inner Hebrides. *Proc. Roy. Soc. Edinb.* 83B, 648pp.

Boyd, J. M. & Jewell, P. A. (1974). The Soay sheep and their environment: a synthesis. In *Island Survivors*, eds. P. A. Jewell, C. Milner & J. M. Boyd, pp. 360–373. Athlone Press, London.

Bramwell, A. G. & Cowie, G. M. (1983). Forests of the Inner Hebrides—Status and habitat. *Proc. Roy. Soc. Edinb.* 83B, 577–597.

Bray, E. (1986). *The Discovery of the Hebrides.* Collins, London.

Brook, A. J. (1964). The phytoplankton of the Scottish freshwater lochs. In *The Vegetation of Scotland* ed. J. H. Burnett. Oliver & Boyd, Edinburgh.

Budge, D. (1960). *Jura, an island of Argyll: its History, People and Story.* John Smith, Bristol.

Burnett, J. H. (1964). *The Vegetation of Scotland.* Oliver & Boyd, Edinburgh.

Cadbury, C. J. (1980). The status and habitats of the corncrake in Britain 1978–79. *Bird Study* 27, 203–218.

Cadbury, C. J. (1988). Corncrake and corn bunting status and habitats on Tiree and Coll, Inner Hebrides. In *Birds of Coll and Tiree* (ed. D. A. Stroud). Nature Conservancy Council, Peterborough.

Caird, J. B. (1988). Landuse in the Uists since 1800. *Proc. Roy. Soc. Edinb.* 77B, 505–526.

Cameron, A. G. (1923). *The Wild Red Deer of Scotland.* Blackwood, London.

Campbell, J. L. ed. (1958). *Gaelic Words and Expressions from South Uist and Eriskay.* Dublin Institute for Advanced Studies.

Campbell, J. L. (1970 et seq.). Macrolepidoptera Cannae. *Entomologist's Rec.* 82, 1–27.

Campbell, J. L. (1984). *Canna— The Story of a Hebridean island.* Oxford University Press, Oxford.

Campbell, J. L. & Thompson, D. S. (1963). *Edward Lhuyd in the Scottish Highlands 1699–1700.* Clarendon, Oxford.

Campbell, M. S. (1945). *The Flora of Uig (Lewis).* Buncle, Arbroath.

Carmichael, A., Watson, J. C. & Matheson, A. (1900 et seq.) 6 vols. *Carmina Gadelica.* Edinburgh.

Clutton-Brock, T. H., Guinness, F. E. & Albon, S. D. (1982). Red deer: behaviour and ecology of two sexes. Chicago and Edinburgh University Presses.

Clutton-Brock, T. H., Guinness, F. E. & Albon, S. D. (1988). Red deer in the Highlands. Blackwell, Oxford.

Clutton-Brock, T. H. & Ball, M. E. (ed.) (1987). Rhum: The Natural History of an Island. Edinburgh University Press.

Cobham Resource Consultants (1987). *An Environmental Assessment of Fish Farms.* CCS, CEC, HIDB & SSGA.

Cockburn, A. M. (1935). Geology of St Kilda. *Trans. Roy. Soc. Edinb.* 58 (21), 511–548.

Craig, G. Y. (1983). ed. *Geology of Scotland.* Scottish Academic Press.

Crown Estate (1987). Fish Farming: guidelines on siting and designing of marine fish farms in Scotland. CEC, Edinburgh.

Cunningham, W. A. J. (1983). *Birds of the Outer Hebrides.* Methuen, Perth.

Currie, A. (1979). The vegetation of the Outer Hebrides. *Proc. Roy. Soc. Edinb.* 77B, 219–265.

Currie, A. & Murray, C. (1983). Flora and vegetation of the Inner Hebrides. *Proc. Roy. Soc. Edinb.* 83B, 293–318.

Darling, F. F. (1937). *A Herd of Red Deer.* Oxford University Press.

Darling, F. F. (1938). *Bird Flocks and the Breeding Cycle.* Cambridge University Press.

Darling, F. F. (1939). *A Naturalist on Rona.* Clarendon Press, Oxford.

Darling, F. F. (1940). *Island Years.* Bell, London.

Darling, F. F. (1944). *Island Farm.* Bell, London.

Darling, F. F. (1945). *Crofting Agriculture.* Oliver & Boyd.

Darling, F. F. (1947). *Natural History of the Highlands and Islands.* Collins, London.

Darling, F. F. (1955). *West Highland Survey: an essay in human ecology.* Oxford University Press.

Darling, F. F. & Boyd, J. M. (1964). *The Highlands and Islands.* Collins, London.

Darwin, C. R. (1859). *On the Origin of Species by Means of Natural Selection.* John Murray, London.

Devine, T. (1988). *The Great Potato Famine in the Highlands.* John Donald, Edinburgh.

Dobson, R. H. & Dobson, R. M. (1985). The natural history of the Muck Islands, N. Ebudes. 1. Introduction and vegetation with a list of vascular plants. *Glasg. Nat.* 21, 13–38.

Dobson, R. H. & Dobson, R. M. (1986). The natural history of the Muck Islands, N. Ebudes. 3. Seabirds and wildfowl. *Glasg. Nat.* 21, 183–199.

Druce, G. C. (1932). *The Comital Flora of the British Isles.* Buncle, Arbroath.

Dwelly, E. (1977). ninth ed. *The Illustrated Gaelic-English Dictionary.* Gairm, Glasgow.

Earll, R., James, G., Lumb, C. & Pagett, R. (1984). The effects of fish farming on the marine environment. Report to the NCC by Marine Biological Consultant.

Elton, C. S. (1938). Note on the ecological and natural history of Pabbay. *J. Ecol.* 26, 275–297.

Elton, C. S. (1949). Population

interspersion: an assay on animal community patterns. *J. Ecol.* 26, 275–297.

Emeleus, C. H. (1980). *1:20,000 Solid geology map of Rhum.* Nature Conservancy Council.

Emeleus, C. H. (1983). Tertiary igneous activity. In *Geology of Scotland.* ed. G. Y. Craig. Scottish Academic Press, Edinburgh.

Ewing, P. (1887–95). A contribution to the topographic botany of the west of Scotland. *Proc. Trans. Nat. Hist. Soc. Glasg.* 2, 309–321; 3, 159–165; 4, 199–214.

Ewing, P. (1892, 1899). The Glasgow catalogue of native and established plants; etc. 1st & 2nd eds. Ewing, Glasgow.

Farrow, G. E. (1983). Recent sediments and sedimentation in the Inner Hebrides. *Proc. Roy. Soc. Edinb.* 83B, 91–105.

Ferreira, R. E. C. (1967). Community descriptions in field survey of vegetation map of the Isle of Rhum. Unpubl. report to Nature Conservancy.

Fisher, J. (1948). St Kilda: a natural experiment. *New Nat. J.*, 91–109.

Fisher, J. (1952). *The Fulmar.* Collins, London.

Fletcher, W. W. & Kirkwood, R. C. ed. (1982) Bracken in Scotland. *Proc. Roy. Soc. Edinb.* 81B, 1–143.

Forbes, A. R. (1905). Gaelic names of beasts (mammalia), birds, fishes, insects, reptiles, etc. Oliver & Boyd, Edinburgh.

Forest, J. E., Waterston, A. R. & Watson, E. V. (1936). The natural history of Barra, Outer Hebrides. *Proc. Roy. Phys. Soc. Edinb.* 22, 41–96.

Gimmingham, C. H. (1964). Maritime and sub-maritime communities. In *The Vegetation of Scotland* ed. J. H. Burnett, Oliver & Boyd, Edinburgh.

Gordon, S. (1926). *The Immortal Isles.* Williams & Norgate, London.

Gordon, S. (1950). *Afoot in the Hebrides.* Country Life, London.

Gowen, R., Brown, J., Bradbury, N. & McLusky, D. S. (1988). Investigations into the benthic enrichment, hypernutrification and eutrophication asociated with mariculture in Scottish coastal waters, 1984–88. Report to the HIDB, CEC, NCC, CCS & SSGA.

Graham, H. D. (1890). *The Birds of Iona and Mull.* Douglas, Edinburgh.

Gray, R. (1871). The Birds of the West of Scotland including the Outer Hebrides. Murray, Glasgow.

Gribble, C. D. (1983). Mineral resources of the Inner Hebrides. *Proc. Roy. Soc. Edinb.* 83B, 611–625.

Harvie-Brown, J. A. & Buckley, T. E. (1888). *A Vertebrate Fauna of the Outer Hebrides.* Douglas, Edinburgh.

Harvie-Brown, J. A. & Buckley, T. E. (1892). *A Vertebrate Fauna of Argyll and the Inner Hebrides.* Douglas, Edinburgh.

Harvie-Brown, J. A. & Macpherson, H. A. (1904). *A Vertebrate Fauna of the North-West Highlands and Skye.* Douglas, Edinburgh.

Henderson, D. M. & Faulkner, R. ed. (1987). Sitka spruce. *Proc. Roy. Soc. Edinb.* 93B, 234pp.

Heron, R. (1794). *General View of the Hebudae or Hebrides.* Patterson, Edinburgh.

Heslop-Harrison, J. W. (1937 and 1939). In *Proc. Univ. Durham Phil. Soc.* The flora of Raasay and adjoining islands, etc. 9, 260–304; the flora of Rhum, Eigg, Canna, Sanday, Muck, Eilein nan Each, Hyskeir, Soay, Pabbay, 10, 87–123; *et al.* (1941) the flora of Coll, Tiree & Gunna, 10, 274–308.

Hewer, H. R. (1974). *British Seals.* Collins, London.

Hiscock, S. (1988). Hidden depths. *Scottish Marine Life*, 1988, 55–58.

Hogan, F. E., Hogan, J. & Macerlean, J. C. (1900). *Irish and Scottish Gaelic Names of Herbs, Plants, Trees, etc.* Gill and Son, Dublin.

Hunter, J. (1976). *The Making of the Crofting Community.* John Donald, Edinburgh.

Jefferies, D. J., Green, J. & Green, R. (1984). *Commercial fish and crustacean traps: a serious cause of otter (Lutra Lutra L.) mortality in Britain and Europe.* 31pp. The Vincent Wildlife Trust, London.

Jeffereys, J. G. (1879–84). On the mollusca procured during the 'Lightning' and 'Porcupine' expeditions. *Proc. Zool. Soc. Lond.* Parts III to VIII.

Jehu, T. J. & Craig, R. M. (1923–24). Geology of the Outer Hebrides. *Trans. Roy. Soc. Edinb.* 53, 419–441, 615–641; 54, 467–489; 55, 457–488; 57, 839–874.

Jenkins, D. (1986). *Trees & Wildlife in the Scottish Uplands.* Institute of Terrestrial Ecology, Banchory.

Jewell, P. A., Milner, C. & Boyd, J. M. eds. (1974). *Island Survivors: the ecology of the Soay sheep of St Kilda*. Athlone Press, London.

Johnson, S. (1924). *Journey to the Western Islands of Scotland* (1773). Oxford University Press.

Kearton, R. & Kearton, C. (1897). *With Nature and a Camera*. Cassell, London.

Kerr, A. J. & Boyd, J. M. (1983). Nature conservation in the Inner Hebrides. *Proc. Roy. Soc. Edinb.* 83B, 627–648.

Kruuk, H. & Hewson, R. (1978). Spacing and foraging of otters (*Lutra lutra*) in a marine habitat, *J. Zool. Lond.* 185, 205–212.

Lhuyd, E. (1707). *Archaelogia Britannica*. London.

Lightfoot, J. (1777). *Flora Scotia*. White, London.

Lindsay, R. A., Riggall, J. & Bignal, E. M. (1983). Ombrogenous mires in Islay and Mull. *Proc. Roy. Soc. Edinb.* 83B, 341–371.

Love, J. A. (1983a). *Return of the sea-eagle*. Cambridge University Press.

Macaulay, K. (1764). *The History of St Kilda*. London.

MacCulloch, J. (1819 & 1824). *A Description of the Western Isles of Scotland*. London.

Macgillivray, W. (1830). Account of the series of islands usually denominated the Outer Hebrides. *J. Nat. Geogr. Sci.* 1, 245–250, 401–411; 2, 87–95, 160–165, 321–334.

Mackenzie, O. H. (1924). *A Hundred Years in the Highlands*. Edward Arnold, London.

Mackie, E. W. (1965). Brochs and the Hebridean Iron Age. *Antiquity* 39, 266–278.

Macleod, A. (1952). *The Songs of Duncan Ban Macintyre*. Oliver & Boyd, Edinburgh.

MacLeoid, R. & MacThomais, R. (1976). *Bith-Eolas*. Gairm, Glaschu.

Maitland, P. S. (1987). *The impact of farmed salmon on the genetics of wild stocks*. Report to Nature Conservancy Council.

Marshall, J. T. (1896–1912). Additions to 'British Conchology'. *J. Conch. Lond.* Vols. 9–13.

Martin, M. (1703). A description of the Western Isles of Scotland. Bell, London.

Mason, J., Shelton, R. G. J., Drinkwater, J. & Howard, F. G. (1983). Shellfish resources in the Inner Hebrides. *Proc. Roy. Soc. Edinb.* 83B, 599–610.

Mather, A. S. & Ritchie, W. (1977). *The Beaches of the Highlands and Islands of Scotland*. Countryside Commission for Scotland.

McIntosh, W. C. (1866). Observations on the marine zoology of North Uist. *Proc. Roy. Soc. Edinb.* 5, 600–614.

McVean, D. N. & Ratcliffe, D. A. (1962). *Plant Communities of the Scottish Highlands*. Nature Conservancy Monograph No. 1. HMSO, Edinburgh.

Menzies, W. J. M. (1938). The movement of salmon marked in the sea, II—Island of Soay and Ardnamurchan in 1938. *Rep. Fishery Bd. Scotl. VII*.

Meteorological Office (1938). *Scotland's Climate*. Meteorological Office, Edinburgh.

Miller, H. (1858). *The Cruise of the Betsey*. Nimmo, Edinburgh.

Mills, D. H. & Graesser, N. (1981). *The Salmon Rivers of Scotland*. Cassell, London.

Mitchell, R., Earll, R. C. & Dipper, F. A. (1983). Shallow sub-littoral ecosystems in the Inner Hebrides. *Proc. Roy. Soc. Edinb.* 83B, 161–184.

Monro, D. (1884). Description of the Western Isles of Scotland (Circa 1549). Thomas D. Morrison, Glasgow.

Mowle, A. D. (1980). *The use of natural resources in the Scottish Highlands, with particular reference to the island of Mull*. PhD Thesis: University of Stirling.

Murray, J. & Pullar, L. (1910). Bathymetrical survey of the Scottish freshwater lochs. *Rep. Scient, Results Bathymetr. Surv. Scot. Freshw. Lochs* 2, 183–221; 6, 68–69.

Murray, W. H. (1973). *The Islands of Western Scotland*. Eyre Methuen, London.

National Trust for Scotland (1979). *St Kilda Handbook* ed. A. Small. NTS, Edinburgh.

Nature Conservancy Council (1974). *Isle of Rhum National Nature Reserve Handbook*. NCC, Edinburgh.

Nature Conservancy Council (1988). *Flow Country: the Peatlands of Caithness and Sutherland* ed. D. A. Ratcliffe & P. H. Oswald. NCC, Edinburgh.

Nature Conservancy Council (1989). *Fish Farming and the Safeguard in the Natural Marine Environment*. NCC, Edinburgh.

Nature Conservancy Council (1989). *Guidelines for Selection of Biological SSSIs*.

Nature Conservacy Council,
Peterborough.

Nicholson, E. M. (1988). *The New Environmental Age*. Cambridge University Press.

Nicolaisen, W. F. H. (1976). *Scottish Place Names: Their Study and Significance*. Batsford, London.

Norton, T. A. & Powell, H. T. (1979). Seaweeds and rocky shores of the Outer Hebrides. *Proc. Roy. Soc. Edinb.* 77B, 141–154.

Ogilvie, M. A. (1983a). Wildlife on Islay. *Proc. Roy. Soc. Edinb.* 83B, 473–489.

Pankhurst, R. J. & Mullin, J. M. (1991). *Flora of the Outer Hebrides*. H.M.S.O. London.

Pearsall, W. H. (1950). *Mountains and Moorlands*. Collins, London.

Pennant (1774–76). *A Tour of Scotland and a Voyage in the Hebrides*. Monk, Chester.

Powell, H. T., Holme, N. A., Knight, S. J. T., Harvey, T., Bishop, G. and Bartrop, J. (1979). *Survey of the littoral zone of the coast of Great Britain, 3, Report on the shores of the Outer Hebrides*. Report to the Nature Conservancy Council.

Powell, H. T., Holme, N. A., Knight, S. J. T., Harvey, T., Bishop, G. and Bartrop, J. (1980). *Survey of the littoral zone of the coast of Great Britain, 6, Report on the shores of Northwest Scotland*. Report to the Nature Conservancy Council.

Ratcliffe, D. A. (ed.) (1977). *A Nature Conservation Review*. Cambridge University Press.

Red Deer Commission (1961–75). *Annual Reports*. RDC, Inverness Press.

Reed, T. M., Currie, A. & Love, J. A. (1983). Birds of the Inner Hebrides. *Proc. Roy. Soc. Edinb.* 83B, 449–472.

Ritchie, J. (1930). Scotland's testimony to the march of evolution. *Scot. Nat.* 1930, 161–169.

Ritchie, J. E. (1932). Tertiary ring structures in Britain. *Trans. Geol. Soc. Glasgow* 19, 42–140.

Royal Commissiion on the Ancient and Historical Monuments of Scotland (1928). *The Outer Hebrides, Skye and the Small Isles*.

Scottish Natural Heritage (1996). Natura 2000, SPAs, Perth.

Scottish Wildlife & Countryside Link (1988). *Marine Fishfarming in Scotland*. AW&CL, Perth.

Scottish Sea Fisheries Statistical Tables 1976–1986. HMSO, Edinburgh.

Sheail, J. (1987). *Seventy-five Years in Ecology*. The British Ecological Society. Blackwell, Oxford.

Sibbald, Sir R. (1684). *Scotia Illustrata*.

Skene, W. F. (1886–90). *Celtic Scotland*, 3 vols, Edinburgh.

Smout, T. C. (1969). *A History of the Scottish People*. Collins, London.

Smout, T. C. (1986). *A Century of Scottish People 1830–1950*. Collins, London.

Statistical Account of Scotland (Old) (1791–99). Edinburgh.

Statistical Account of Scotland (New) (1845). Blackwoods, Edinburgh.

Steel, T. (1975). *The Life and Death of St Kilda*. Fontana, London.

Steel, W. O. & Woodroffe, G. E. (1969). The entomology of the Isle of Rhum National Nature Reserve. *Trans. Soc. Brit. Entomol.* 18, 91–167.

Stewart, M. (1933). *Ronay*. Oxford University Press.

Stewart, M. (1937). *St Kilda Papers 1931*. Private publ.

St John, C. (1884). *A Tour of Sutherlandshire*. 2 vols. Douglas, Edinburgh.

St John, C. (1893). *Short Sketches of the Wild Sports and Natural History of the Highlands*. J. Murray, London.

Storrie, M. C. (1981). *Islay: Biography of an Island*. Oa Press, Isle of Islay.

Stowe, T. J. & Hudson, A. V. (1988). Corncrake studies in the Western Isles. *RSPB Conservation Review*. 1988, 38–42.

Sulloway, F. J. (1984). Darwin and the Galapagos. *Biol. J. Linn. Soc.* 21, 29–60.

Sykes, E. R. (1906–25). In the mollusca procured during the 'Porcupine' expeditions 1869–70. *Proc. Malac. Soc. Lond.* Parts III, IV, V.

Taylor, C. S. (1981). *Status and habitats available for vertebrates in forests in the Inner Hebrides*. Report to the Forestry Commission.

Thompson, D. S. (1983). *The Companion to Gaelic Scotland*. Blackwell, Oxford.

Trail, J. W. H. (1898–1909). Topographical botany of Scotland (followed by additions and corrections). *Ann. Scot. Nat. Hist.* 1898–1900; 1905–1909.

Twelves, J. (1983). Otter (*Lutra lutra*) mortalities in lobster creels. *J. Zool. Lond.* 201, 285–288.

Waterston, A. R. (1981). Present knowledge of the non-marine invertebrate fauna of the Outer Hebrides. *Proc. Roy. Soc. Edinb.* 77B, 215–321.

Waterston, A. R. & Lyster, I. H. J. (1979). The macrofauna of brackish and freshwaters and of the Loch Druidibeg National Nature Reserve and its neighbourhood, South Uist. *Proc. Roy. Soc. Edinb.* 77B, 353–376.

Watson, H. C. (1873–74). *Topographic Botany.* 1st ed. London. 2nd ed. 1883.

Watson, J. (1983). Lewisian. In *Geology of Scotland.* Ed. G. Y. Craig. Scottish Academic Press, Edinburgh.

Watson, W. J. (1926). *The History of the Celtic Place-names of Scotland.* Blackwood, Edinburgh.

Welch, R. C. (1983). Coleoptera in the Inner Hebrides. *Proc. Roy. Soc. Edinb.* 83B, 505–529.

Williamson, K. & Boyd, J. M. (1960). *St Kilda Summer.* Hutchinson, London.

Williamson, K. & Boyd, J. M. (1963). *Mosaic of Islands.* Oliver & Boyd, Edinburgh.

Wormell, P. (1977). Woodland insect population changes in the Isle of Rhum in relation to forest history and woodland restoration. *Scott. Forest.* 31, 13–36.

Wormell, P. (1983). Lepidoptera in the Inner Hebrides. *Proc. Roy. Soc. Edinb.* 83B, 531–546.

Index